Praise for A Fa

MW00770921

"*A Father Offers His Son* will stimulate your mind and encourage your soul. You will be refreshed by the analysis of this familiar account from Genesis 22. This book has good theology and is a wonderful, enjoyable read. There are excellent insights about that event on Mount Moriah, and they will challenge your thinking. This work lifts up our Lord Jesus Christ, and it will deepen your appreciation for what He and the Father went through to bring us back into fellowship. I highly recommend it."

   Dr. Paul Benware—Professor of Bible and Theology at Moody Bible Institute and the Master's University, Pastor, Conference Speaker, and Author

"Abraham's intended sacrifice of Isaac is a rare and poignant picture of the unfathomable cost to the Father who sacrificed His Son for us. This book is a wonderful and touching treatment of that passage. As a jeweler holds a gemstone in the light and turns it slowly examining each priceless, shining facet, Scott LaPierre holds high this picture of heaven's sacrificial love, and he slowly, unhurriedly, examines its every detail. *A Father Offers His Son* is beautifully biblical, incredibly insightful, and remarkably readable."

   Cary Green—Speaker, Missionary, Church Planter, and Senior Pastor of Cornerstone Bible Church

A FATHER OFFERS HIS SON

A FATHER OFFERS HIS SON

The True and Greater Sacrifice Revealed Through Abraham and Isaac

Scott LaPierre

www.scottlapierre.org | scott@scottlapierre.org

ISBN 10: 0-9995551-1-1
ISBN 13: 978-0-9995551-1-8
Library of Congress Control Number: 2018910332
Charis Publishing

Unless otherwise indicated all Scripture quotations are taken from the New King James Version®. Copyright © 1982 by Thomas Nelson. Used by permission. All rights reserved.

Abbreviations used for other versions:

- ESV—The ESV® Bible copyright © 2001 by Crossway, a publishing ministry of Good News Publishers. ESV® Text Edition: 2011.
- NASB—Scripture taken from the NEW AMERICAN STANDARD BIBLE®, Copyright © 1960, 1962, 1963, 1968, 1971, 1972, 1973, 1975, 1977, 1995 by The Lockman Foundation.
- NIV—THE HOLY BIBLE, NEW INTERNATIONAL VERSION®, NIV® Copyright © 1973, 1984, 2011 by Biblica, Inc. ®

Scripture quotations with brackets, parentheses, or italics are the emphasis of the author.

Dedication

A Father Offers His Son is dedicated to Elwyn Ordway.

God used you to share the gospel with me following my brother's death. Although I knew religion, I did not know Jesus until you came into my life.

I will always be thankful for you.

Love your friend and brother in Christ,
Scott

Acknowledgments

First, I want to thank Kandie Schmitz, Stacy Mouat, and Marcus Taylor for your service as beta readers. Pastor Cary and Lois Green, thank you for going above and beyond as readers and friends. Pam Lagomarsino, I am blessed to have found you as an editor, and I hope to keep you busy for years to come.

Second, I want to thank the wonderful congregation at Woodland Christian Church. This book came from sermons I preached, and your hunger for God's Word encouraged me in my studying each week.

Finally, I want to thank my Lord and Savior, Jesus Christ, for the privilege of writing about Your love and sacrifice. You are the true and greater reality (Hebrews 10:1 ESV) and substance (Colossians 2:17) of all types and shadows.

Table of Contents

Introduction

I became a Christian in my early twenties. Soon after, I started reading the Bible for the first time. Like many people, I began "in the beginning" at Genesis 1:1. I read some accounts I was already familiar with: creation, the fall, Cain and Abel, and the flood. I did not struggle with much of what I read, not even the destruction of Sodom and Gomorrah. Then everything came to a screeching halt when I read Genesis 22:1–2:

> Now it came to pass after these things that God
> tested Abraham, and said to him, "Abraham!"
> And he said, "Here I am."
> Then He said, "Take now your son, your only son
> Isaac, whom you love, and go to the land of
> Moriah, and offer him there as a burnt offering on
> one of the mountains of which I shall tell you."

I thought, "God made Abraham wait so long for this son. Why would He then make such a cruel request? I can understand God calling down fire on Sodom and Gomorrah, but how could He ask Abraham to sacrifice his own son?" As a new Christian, I did not understand. After careful studying, I realized God did not intend for Abraham to sacrifice Isaac. We know that because the

Angel stopped him: "Do not lay your hand on the lad, or do anything to him (Genesis 22:12a)." If God did not want Abraham to sacrifice Isaac, then what did He want? The answer is twofold.

First, He wanted to test Abraham. We read that in the first verse of the chapter. God's request had never been anything but a test—not to see Abraham sacrifice Isaac, but to see whether Abraham would do it. When Abraham revealed he would obey God's command, the Angel stopped him. Abraham passed the test, and there was no reason for it to continue.

Second, God wanted a picture of what He would do with His Son two thousand years later. He wants us to understand the sacrifice He made, so He put it in human terms. Twice the Angel of the LORD commended Abraham for not withholding his son:

- Genesis 22:12b—[He] said, "For now I know that you fear God, since *you have not withheld your son,* your only son, from Me."
- Genesis 22:16—[He] said, "Because you have done this thing, and *have not withheld your son*, your only son."

God had no intention of Abraham sacrificing Isaac, but this account looked forward to what God had every intention of doing with Jesus. Abraham did not spare his son but was willing to deliver him up, and Romans 8:32 says, "[God] *did not spare His own Son, but delivered Him up* for us all, how shall He not with Him also freely give us all things?"

Let me make three requests for you to keep in mind as you read *A Father Offers His Son*...

First, God wants us to appreciate His love for us. So, as you read consider how hard this was for Abraham. When you put yourself in Abraham's place, you develop some idea of how heart-wrenching it was for God. Do you have a son? What if God made this request of you? As you read about the sacrifice Abraham was willing to make, think on the even greater sacrifice God was willing to make and why He was willing to make it—His great love for us: "God demonstrates His own love toward us, in that while we were still sinners, Christ died for us" (Romans 5:8).

Second, Jesus wants us to appreciate the sacrifice He made for us. So think of what it was like for Isaac. When you put yourself in Isaac's place, you can identify with how hard it was for Jesus. What if you received the same request Isaac received? As you consider the sacrifice Isaac was willing to become, reflect on the even greater sacrifice Jesus became. In John 15:13, Jesus said, "Greater love has no one than this, than to lay down one's life for his friends."

Third, keep this analogy in mind so you do not "settle for scraps." Imagine that you prepare a delicious feast for your friends, but when they arrive, they sit on the floor and eat the crumbs that fall from the table. If you read the account of Abraham and Isaac and fail to see God the

Father and His Son, you are eating the crumbs. You have missed the wonderful feast that has been prepared for you.

Genesis 22 is not primarily about Abraham and Isaac. Yes, they are present, but you want to see the true and greater Father and Son in the story. John 12:20–21 says:

> Now there were certain Greeks among those who came up to worship at the feast. Then they came to Philip, who was from Bethsaida of Galilee, and asked him, saying, *"Sir, we wish to see Jesus."*

Desiring to see Jesus should be our hearts' cry! My desire for you as you read this book is that you see Jesus and that by seeing Him, you grow in your love and thankfulness for Him.

Chapter 1

The Old Testament
Is about Jesus

Many people search for Jesus. In the Bible, we have an account of someone finding Him and recognizing He is the Messiah. The person was Philip and he wanted his friend, Nathaniel, to meet Him too. When Philip spoke to Nathaniel, he revealed why he thought Jesus was the Messiah: "We have found Him of whom Moses in the law, and also the Prophets, wrote— Jesus of Nazareth, the son of Joseph." (John 1:45). The "Law and the Prophets" was a title for the Old Testament before the New Testament was written. Philip understood the Old Testament was about Jesus, which is why he believed Jesus was the Messiah. He expected Nathaniel to be convinced He was the Messiah as well because he would also recognize Him as the One identified in the Law and the Prophets.

Jesus also said the Old Testament is about Him:

- Luke 24:27—"Beginning at Moses and all the Prophets, [Jesus] expounded to them in all the Scriptures the things concerning Himself."
- Luke 24:44—"[Jesus] said, 'All things must be fulfilled which were written in the Law of Moses and the Prophets and the Psalms concerning Me.'"
- Hebrews 10:7—"[Jesus said,] 'Behold, I have come—in the volume of the book it is written of Me.'"

How is the Old Testament about Jesus? He is primarily revealed in two ways. First, there are prophecies of Him. For example these verses state He would:

- Be from the tribe of Judah (Genesis 49:10)
- Receive King David's throne (2 Samuel 7:12–13)
- Be spat upon and beaten (Isaiah 50:6)
- Be silent in the face of accusations (Isaiah 53:7)
- Spend a season in Egypt (Hosea 11:1)
- Ride into Jerusalem on a donkey (Zechariah 9:9)

And the list goes on. And on. And on. Jesus fulfilled around 350 prophecies in His first coming.[1]

The second way the Old Testament reveals Jesus is through types or shadows:

- Hebrews 10:1 says, "The law [was only] a shadow of the good things to come instead of the true form of these realities" (ESV).
- Colossians 2:16–17 says a "festival or a new moon or sabbaths [are] a shadow of things to come, but the substance is of Christ."

"Shadows" are a fitting way to describe the types of Christ in the Old Testament because shadows provide an idea of what something looks like without completely revealing the object. The Old Testament does this with Christ. A shadow is evidence that something is casting it, or in the case of Christ, it is Someone. Finally, nobody looks at a shadow and believes it is the real thing. Nobody sees the shadow of a tree or car and thinks it is a tree or car. Shadows have no substance. They are not the reality. In Colossians 2:17, Jesus is the substance and in Hebrews 10:1, He is the reality.

The New Testament identifies many types and shadows of Christ in the Old Testament. For example:

- John 3:14 compares Jesus with the Bronze Serpent: "As Moses lifted up the serpent in the wilderness, even so must the Son of Man be lifted up."
- John 6:32–33 compares Jesus with the manna: "Moses did not give you the bread from heaven, but My Father gives you the true bread from heaven. For the bread of God is He who comes down from heaven and gives life to the world."

- Romans 5:14 compares Jesus with Adam: "Adam is a type of Him who was to come."
- First Corinthians 5:7 compares Jesus with the Passover Lamb: "For indeed Christ, our Passover, was sacrificed for us."
- First Corinthians 10:4 compares Jesus with the rock that accompanied Israel in the wilderness: "[Israel] drank of that spiritual Rock that followed them, and that Rock was Christ."
- Hebrews 10:20 compares Jesus' body with the veil in the temple that when "torn" on the cross revealed the access believers have to the Father: "[We have] a new and living way [to God] which [Jesus] consecrated for us, through the veil, [which] is, His flesh."

Certain practices looked forward to Christ. The law commanded sacrifices for sins, and each sacrifice looked forward to Jesus—the true and greater Sacrifice for sins. Circumcision has its fulfillment in Christ because He helps us put off our sinful flesh: "In [Christ] you were circumcised… without hands by putting off… the flesh, by the circumcision of Christ" (Colossians 2:11). Hebrews 4:1–9 says the rest people enjoyed on the Sabbath was a picture of the true and greater rest that is found in Christ.

Miracles in the Old Testament prefigured some miracles Jesus would perform in a greater way:

- Moses unleashed ten judgments on one nation (Exodus 7–12), but Jesus will unleash twenty-one judgments on the whole earth: "And the kings of the earth, the great men, the rich men, the commanders, the mighty men, every slave and every free man, hid themselves in the caves and in the rocks of the mountains, and said to the mountains and rocks, 'Fall on us and hide us from the face of Him who sits on the throne and from the wrath of the Lamb!'" (Revelation 6:15–16).
- God took Elijah up to heaven in a whirlwind (2 Kings 2:11), but Jesus ascended to heaven on His own (Acts 1:9).
- Elisha fed one hundred men with twenty loaves (2 Kings 4:42–44), but Jesus fed 5,000 and 4,000 men with five and seven loaves (Matthew 14:13–21 and 15:32–39).
- Elisha cleansed one man of leprosy (2 Kings 5:1–14), but Jesus cleansed ten men (Luke 17:11–19).
- Elisha knew what Gehazi had done (2 Kings 5:26), but Jesus knows what all men have done (John 2:24).
- Elisha's death gave one person temporary life (2 Kings 13:21), but Jesus' death gives many people eternal life (Romans 5:18).

What is the purpose of all the prophecies and shadows? To lead people to Christ! Jesus said, "All the prophets and the law prophesied until John" (Matthew 11:13). Jesus was veiled throughout the Old Testament in the types and shadows, but when John the Baptist arrived as Jesus' forerunner, He was no longer veiled. John pointed at Him and said, "Behold! The Lamb of God Who takes away the sin of the world!" (John 1:29).

The Old Testament Serves as a Treasure Map

Paul asked a question many people would answer incorrectly:

Galatians 3:19a—"What purpose then does the law serve?"

Typical answers would be something like, "To show you how to be a good person," or "To help you get to heaven." The law serves the opposite purpose! Instead of showing us how to be good, it shows us we are *not* good. When we become familiar with the law and see what it requires to be "good"—or righteous—we see we "have sinned and fall short of the glory of God" (Romans 3:23).

Galatians 3:19b—"It was added because of transgressions, till the Seed (Jesus) should come…"

The New Testament was written in Greek, and the word for "transgression" is *parabasis*, which means, "going over."[2] People transgress when they know where God has drawn the line, but they step over it anyway. Although, people can only transgress if they know where the line is drawn. The law reveals the line, and thereby also our transgressions. Romans 3:20 says, "for by the law *is the knowledge of sin.*" The law helps us see our need for a Savior by revealing our sinfulness to us. When we look at the standard the law sets, we see how far short we fall from keeping it.

Romans 5:20 says "the law entered that the offense might abound." This does not mean God gave the law so we would sin more. Instead, God gave the law so our sins would become clear. They would seem to be "abounding" or springing up around us. In Romans 7:7, Paul said, "I would not have known sin except through the law. For I would not have known covetousness unless the law had said, 'You shall not covet.'" Paul did not know he was sinning until he learned the law said not to covet!

We naturally think we are good. Proverbs 16:2 and 21:2 say, "All the ways of a man are pure in his own eyes," and Proverbs 30:12 says, "There is a generation that is pure in its own eyes, yet is not washed from its filthiness." How could filthy people think they are pure? They are not familiar with God's law that would reveal their filthiness to them. Jeremiah had one of the most painful ministries in Scripture because he addressed sinful people who thought they were good. Notice his and God's efforts at reaching them:

- Jeremiah 2:23—[Jeremiah said], "How can you say, 'I am not polluted, I have not gone after the Baals'? See your way in the valley; know what you have done: you are a swift dromedary breaking loose in her ways." They thought they were not polluted, but they pursued idols like an animal in heat pursues a mate.

- Jeremiah 2:35—[God said], "Yet you say, 'Because I am innocent, surely His anger shall turn from me.' Behold, I will plead My case against you, because you say, 'I have not sinned.'" God said He would judge them because they were sinners who said they were innocent.

The problem with people who think they are not sinners is they see no need for a Savior. People only want:

- A parachute when they know the plane is crashing
- A cure when they learn they have a disease
- The fire department when they know there is a fire

The law says, "Your plane is crashing... you have a disease... there is a fire!" This is what Jesus meant in Luke 5:31 when He said, "Those who are well have no need of a physician, but those who are sick." People who think they are spiritually healthy do not recognize their need for Jesus. The law can show them they are spiritually sick.

Despite how important the law is, it does not serve the same purpose throughout our lives. Paul says it lasts until we come to faith in Jesus (the Seed).

Galatians 3:23—"But before faith came, we were kept under guard by the law, kept for the faith which would afterward be revealed."

We should not interpret this literally to mean there was a time when there was not faith. Justified means "declared righteous," and the law cannot justify us because we are too sinful to obey it perfectly; therefore, God graciously allows justification to take place by faith. He says to wretched sinners, "Because of your faith in My Son, I will give you His righteousness." Sadly, those unfamiliar with the gospel claim they are righteous because of the way they live, but the way they live only demonstrates their unrighteousness.

Two thousand years before Christ came, Genesis 15:6 says, "[Abraham] believed in the LORD, and He accounted it to him for righteousness." Abraham was justified by faith. Believers in the Old Testament looked forward to Christ's coming like believers in the New Testament look back on Christ's coming. "Before faith" means before people put their faith in Christ. Until then the law "held [them] in custody" (NIV) or "kept [them] captive and imprisoned" (ESV).

Galatians 3:24—"Therefore the law was our tutor to bring us to Christ, that we might be justified by faith."

When people become Christians, the Old Testament served its purpose in being a tutor—or treasure map—that led them to Christ.

Galatians 3:25—"But after faith has come, we are no longer under a tutor."

Just as "before faith came" meant before putting faith in Christ, "after faith has come" means after putting faith in Christ. At that point, we "no longer [need] a tutor," because the law has served its purpose in our lives. The Old Testament served as a map to lead us to the treasure, which is Christ.

Do Not Miss the Treasure

Therefore, if you learned everything the Old Testament could teach—if you could recount every story, recite countless verses—but it did not lead you to Christ, then you have made the same mistake the religious leaders made in Jesus' day. Jesus criticized them saying, "You search the Scriptures, for in them you think you have eternal life; and these are they which testify of Me... If you believed Moses, you would believe Me; for He wrote about Me" (John 5:39, 46). If you miss that the Old Testament testifies of Christ, then you have failed to let it be your tutor.

If you read about Abraham and Isaac, but you fail to see the true and greater Father and Son, then you missed the treasure. You are looking at the shadow of a tree while saying, "Look at that amazing tree!" If you read Genesis 22 and only see Abraham and Isaac, in the language of

Hebrews 10:1, you are missing the "reality," which is Christ. In the language of Colossians 2:17 you are overlooking the "substance" we find in Christ.

Questions

1. Why did Jesus say the Old Testament is about Him?

2. Why is it fitting to call Old Testament types of Christ shadows?

3. What purpose(s) does the law serve?

Chapter 2

Genesis 22:2–3
Isaac and Jesus Were... Part I

Isaac and Jesus Were Only Begotten Sons

Genesis 22:2—"Then He said, 'Take now your son, *your only son* Isaac, whom you love, and go to the land of Moriah, and offer him there as a burnt offering on one of the mountains of which I shall tell you.'"

The typology between Isaac and Jesus is immediately established strongly. The language used regarding Abraham and Isaac is almost identical to the language used in the New Testament regarding God the Father and His Son. In Genesis 22:2 God said to Abraham, "your son, your only son." He repeated these words two more times:

- Genesis 22:12—"And He said, 'Do not lay your hand on the lad, or do anything to him; for now I know that you fear God, since you have not withheld your son, *your only son*, from Me.'"
- Genesis 22:16—[The Angel of the LORD] said: "By Myself I have sworn, says the LORD, because you have done this thing, and have not withheld your son, *your only son*."

God does not waste words in Scripture. When He is repetitive, it is for a reason. God does not use highlighting, italics, underlining, or bold for emphasis, but He does repeat Himself when He wants to ensure we do not miss something. God wants us to recognize Isaac was, "[Abraham's] son, [his] only son." Abraham had another son, Ishmael, so how can God refer to Isaac as Abraham's "only" son? The word "only" does not mean "single." The Old Testament has three Hebrew words for "only." Here are two of them:

1. Genesis 6:5—"Then the LORD saw that the wickedness of man was great in the earth, and that every intent of the thoughts of his heart was only [*raq*] evil continually."[3]
2. Genesis 7:23—"So He destroyed all living things which were on the face of the ground: both man and cattle, creeping thing and bird of the air. They were destroyed from the earth. Only [*'ak*] Noah and those who were with him in the ark remained alive."[4]

The Old Testament is primarily written in Hebrew (with small portions written in Aramaic), and the word for "only" in Genesis 22:2 is *yachiyd*, which means "unique."[5] It is referring to Isaac being Abraham's special, one-of-a-kind son. The same word is translated as "precious" elsewhere in Scripture:

- Psalm 22:20—"Deliver Me from the sword, My precious [yachiyd] life from the power of the dog."
- Psalm 35:17—"Rescue me from their destructions, My precious [yachiyd] life from the lions."

The *Theological Wordbook of the Old Testament* (TWOT) says yachiyd means, "only begotten son."[6] This makes Isaac look like Jesus, the only begotten Son of God. "Begotten" does not mean "created." The writers of the Nicene Creed wanted to make sure nobody misunderstood the word, so they said:

I believe… in one Lord Jesus Christ, the only-begotten Son of God, begotten of the Father before all worlds; God of God, Light of Light, very God of very God; begotten, *not made*, being of one substance with the Father, by Whom all things were made.[7]

The creed teaches Jesus is eternal, and as the Son of God, is equal with God. If begotten does not mean created, what does it mean? The Greek word for "only begotten" is *monogenes*, and it means, "single of its kind."[8] Again, it means Jesus is God's unique Son. This separates Him from believers who are sons and daughters of God by adoption, and angels who are also called "sons of God" (Genesis 6:4, Job 1:6, 2:1, 38:7 cf. Hebrews 1:5–14). Monogenes only occurs nine times in Scripture:

- Three times Luke used the word to describe parents who lost an "only" (monogenes) child (Luke 7:12, 8:42, and 9:38).
- Five times John used the word to refer to Jesus as "the only begotten (monogenes) Son" (John 1:14, 18, 3:16, 18, 1 John 4:9).

The last use identifies the other individual in Scripture given the same title as Jesus. Hebrews 11:17 says, "By faith Abraham, when he was tested, offered up Isaac… *His only begotten (monogenes) son.*" God asked Abraham to sacrifice Isaac, instead of Ishmael, because He wanted him to sacrifice his only begotten, special, unique, precious son. This looked forward to God sacrificing His only begotten, special, unique, precious Son.

Isaac and Jesus Were Named by God

Genesis 22:2—"Then He said, 'Take now your son, your only son *Isaac*, whom you love, and go to the land of Moriah, and offer him there as a burnt offering on one of the mountains of which I shall tell you.'"

The mention of Isaac's name draws a connection to Jesus. Isaac also had the rare distinction of being named by God, instead of being named by earthly parents. Notice the parallelism between these verses:

- Genesis 17:19—"Sarah… shall bear you a son, and you shall call his name Isaac."
- Matthew 1:21—"[Mary] shall bring forth a Son, and you shall call His name Jesus."

Isaac and Jesus Were Loved by Their Fathers

Genesis 22:2—"Then He said, 'Take now your son, your only son Isaac, *whom you love*, and go to the land of Moriah, and offer him there as a burnt offering on one of the mountains of which I shall tell you.'"

The "Principle of First Mention" encourages Bible scholars to take notice of the first time words are used in the Old and New Testaments, and even in each book of the Bible.[9] The idea is God reveals the truest meaning of a word when it first occurs. Genesis 22:2 contains the first use of the word "love." Considering the different relationships involving love—for example, mother to a son, daughter to a father, sister to a brother, husband to a wife—makes it more significant that the first time the word "love" is in the Old Testament, it describes the love a father feels toward his son.

The first time the word "love" occurs in the New Testament also describes a Father's love for a Son. God's words at Jesus' baptism echo His words to Abraham: "This is My Son, *whom I love*" (Matthew 3:17 NIV). The parallel verses in Mark 1:11 and Luke 3:22 are also the first time the word love is used in each gospel. As Isaac was the object of his father's love toward the beginning of the Old Testament, so too was Jesus the object of His Father's love toward the beginning of the New Testament.

Isaac and Jesus Reveal God's Love for the World

God stated His love for Jesus at the beginning of Matthew, Mark, and Luke; however, a change takes place in John's gospel. The first time John uses the word love he describes God's love, not for His Son, but for the world—a love so great that God was willing to sacrifice the Son He stated His love for in the previous three gospels: "For God so loved the world that He gave His only begotten Son, that whoever believes in Him should not perish but have everlasting life" (John 3:16).

Abraham loved his son, but he was willing to give him up because of his love for God. Similarly, God the Father loved His Son, but He was willing to give Him up because of His love for us.

Isaac and Jesus Were "Offered" Up

Genesis 22:2—"Then He said, 'Take now your son, your only son Isaac, whom you love, and go to the land of Moriah, and *offer him* there as a burnt offering on one of the mountains of which I shall tell you.'"

The Hebrew word for "offered" is *alah,* but it does not mean "given" or "presented" as we would expect. It means, "to go up, ascend, climb, be taken or lifted up."[10] The idea is that when something is sacrificed, it is "lifted" up to God. Of the eight hundred eighty-nine times alah occurs in the Old Testament, six hundred seventy-six times it translates as "up." When Abraham was commanded to "offer" Isaac, he was essentially commanded to "lift him up." Jesus spoke of His sacrifice this way:

- John 3:14—"As Moses lifted up the serpent in the wilderness, even *so must the Son of Man be lifted up."*
- John 12:32—"If *I am lifted up* from the earth, will draw all peoples to Myself."

Isaac and Jesus Were Burnt Offerings

Genesis 22:2—"Then He said, 'Take now your son, your only son Isaac, whom you love, and go to the land of Moriah, and offer him there *as a burnt offering* on one of the mountains of which I shall tell you.'"

God did not just ask Abraham to sacrifice Isaac. He specifically said to "offer him as a burnt offering." Again, God is repetitive to make sure we do not miss this. The words "burnt offering" occur six times between verses two and thirteen. Almost every other verse reminds us Isaac was to be a burnt offering.

Leviticus 1 describes burnt offerings. They were voluntary acts of worship to express devotion to God, or they could serve as an atonement for unintentional sins. The meat, bones, and organs were completely burnt, and this was God's portion. The animal's hide was given to the Levites, who could later sell it to earn money for themselves.

Burnt offerings make a fitting picture of Christ. Three times they are called "an offering made by fire, a sweet aroma to the LORD" (Leviticus 1:9, 13, 17). Paul applies this imagery to Jesus: "[Christ] has given Himself for us, an offering and a sacrifice to God for a sweet-smelling aroma" (Ephesians 5:2). The key verse is Leviticus 1:4. Let's look at it, piece-by-piece:

- Leviticus 1:4a says "[The priest] shall put his hand on the head of the burnt offering." This communicated the transmission of the sin to the sacrifice, and it looked to the way our sins are transmitted to Christ. Isaiah 53:6 says "the LORD has laid on [Jesus] the iniquity of us all." In many pictures of the account, Abraham has the knife in one hand, and his other hand is on Isaac's head to maintain the imagery.
- Leviticus 1:4b says the burnt offering "will be accepted on [the sinner's] behalf" looking to the way Christ died in our place.

- Leviticus 1:4c says the burnt offering will "make atonement for [the sinner]" looking to the way Jesus made atonement for our sins.

Leviticus 6:11 says the priest shall, "carry the ashes [of the burnt offering] outside the camp." Hebrews 13:12–13 uses the same language discussing Christ's sacrifice: "He… suffered *outside the gate*. Therefore let us go forth to Him, *outside the camp*, bearing His reproach." Leviticus 1:9 and 13 say "the priest shall burn all on the altar." Burnt offerings were completely consumed, and Jesus is the true and greater Burnt Offering who was willing to be completely consumed for our sins.

Isaac and Jesus Were Sacrificed In Jerusalem

Genesis 22:2—"Then He said, 'Take now your son, your only son Isaac, whom you love, and go to *the land of Moriah*, and offer him there as a burnt offering *on one of the mountains of which I shall tell you.*'"

Jerusalem has a rich history. It is mentioned six hundred forty-three times in Scripture, which is much more than any other location. This does not even include the times it is called Zion, the City of David, or referenced indirectly. Babylon is second, occurring only two-hundred sixty-two times. Jerusalem is first mentioned in Genesis 14:18 when Melchizedek, the "King of Salem," shows up in Scripture.

"Salem" means "peace," hence Jerusalem being "The City of Peace."

Before the Israelites entered the Promised Land, God told them He would choose a place for Himself: "You shall seek the place where the LORD your God chooses, out of all your tribes, to put His name for His dwelling place; and there you shall go" (Deuteronomy 12:5; also 11, 14, 18, 21, and 26).

The Canaanites controlled the Promised Land when Israel entered it. Since Jebusites inhabited Jerusalem, it was called "Jebus" (Joshua 10:1, 3, 5, 23). Joshua 15:63 says: "As for the Jebusites, the inhabitants of Jerusalem, the children of Israel could not drive them out; but the Jebusites dwell with the children of Judah at Jerusalem to this day."

The Jebusites remained in Jerusalem until David conquered it, drove out the Jebusites, and made it his capital. Second Samuel 5:6–7, 9 records:

> [David] and his men went to Jerusalem against the Jebusites, the inhabitants of the land, who spoke to David, saying, "You shall not come in here; but the blind and the lame will repel you," thinking, "David cannot come in here." Nevertheless David took the stronghold of Zion (that is, the City of David). Then David dwelt in the stronghold, and called it the City of David. And David built all around from the Millo and inward.

While David lived in the palace, he decided God should have His own "house." Second Samuel 7:1–2 records:

Now it came to pass when the king was dwelling in his house, and the LORD had given him rest from all his enemies all around, that the king said to Nathan the prophet, "See now, I dwell in a house of cedar, but the ark of God dwells inside tent curtains."

Although David's desire was good, God told him his son, Solomon, would build the temple instead (2 Samuel 7:13). Second Chronicles 3:1 says:

Then Solomon began to build the house of the LORD in Jerusalem *on Mount Moriah*, where the LORD had appeared to David his father, at the place that David had appointed, on the threshing floor of [Araunah] the Jebusite.[11]

Genesis 22:1 says, "God tested Abraham," and the test was to see whether Abraham would sacrifice his son. Abraham could pass this test anywhere, but God said to "offer [Isaac]... on one of the mountains of which I shall tell you." Consider the following:

- God had Abraham travel fifty miles over three days from Beersheba to Jerusalem.
- God showed Abraham the specific location to sacrifice Isaac.

- The account serves as a picture of what God would later do with His Son.

More than likely the location God revealed to Abraham was Calvary or Golgotha. "Moriah" means, "chosen by Jehovah,"[12] and God chose this location for Abraham to sacrifice Isaac because two thousand years later He would sacrifice His Son on this same mountain:

> The decision of God to establish his temple at Moriah in Jerusalem has affected all history; for this mountain became the focus of the Holy City, where His Son was crucified. And it will continue to affect history; for from this 'city He loves,' He will someday rule the nations of the earth.[13]

Isaac and Jesus Were Accompanied by Two Men on Their Way to Be Sacrificed

Genesis 22:3, 5—So Abraham rose early in the morning and saddled his donkey, *and took two of his young men with him*, and Isaac his son; and he split the wood for the burnt offering, and arose and went to the place of which God had told him... And Abraham said to his young men, "*Stay here with the donkey*; the lad and I will go yonder and worship, and we will come back to you."

Isaac was accompanied by two men on his way to being sacrificed like Jesus was accompanied by two men when

He was sacrificed. Matthew 27:38 says, "Then two robbers were crucified with Him, one on the right and another on the left."

The two men were not able to witness what took place between Abraham and Isaac. Similarly, when Jesus was sacrificed, nobody could see exactly what took place between God the Father and God the Son. When Jesus was on the cross, Matthew 27:45 says, "Now from the sixth hour until the ninth hour there was darkness over all the land." The darkness concealed the divine transaction when our sins were placed on Christ.

Questions

1. List the parallels between Isaac and Jesus found in Genesis 22:2–3.

2. Can you think of any other similarities in these verses between Isaac and Jesus and Abraham and God? If so, what are they?

3. How does Jesus' sacrifice reveal God's love?

Chapter 3

Genesis 22:4–6
Isaac and Jesus Were... Part II

Isaac and Jesus Were
Raised on the Third Day

Genesis 22:4—Then *on the third day* Abraham lifted his eyes and saw the place afar off.

There are clear Old Testament prophecies that Jesus would be raised from the dead. Psalm 16 is a messianic psalm, which means that even though David wrote it, we can read it as though Jesus is speaking. In verse 10, he says, "For You will not leave my soul in Sheol, nor will You allow Your Holy One to see corruption." Peter quotes this verse in Acts 2:27, and Paul quotes it in Acts 13:35 as prophecies of Jesus' resurrection. Isaiah 53:10 also prophesies of Jesus' resurrection:

Yet it pleased the L ORD to bruise Him;
He has put Him to grief.
When You make His soul an offering for sin,
He shall see His seed, He shall prolong His days,
And the pleasure of the Lord shall prosper in His
hand.

Jesus did not have physical children (seed), but He has
spiritual children. Isaiah says He will see these children
after He has been killed—"bruised... put to grief... [made]
an offering." Jesus would die, but the Father would
"prolong His days," referring to His resurrection.

While most Christians know it was prophesied that
Jesus would be raised from the dead on the third day, few
Christians can find the prophecy in the Old Testament.
Why is that? When Jesus fulfilled prophecies, the New
Testament often quotes the Old Testament verse that
contains the prophecy. For example:

- Matthew 1:22–23 references Isaiah 7:14—"So all
  this was done that it might be fulfilled which was
  spoken by the Lord through the prophet, saying:
  'Behold, the virgin shall be with child, and bear a
  Son, and they shall call His name Immanuel,' which
  translates as, 'God with us.'"
- Matthew 2:5–6 references Micah 5:2—So they said
  to him, "In Bethlehem of Judea, for thus it is written
  by the prophet: 'But you, Bethlehem, in the land of
  Judah, are not the least among the rulers of Judah;

> For out of you shall come a Ruler who will shepherd My people Israel.'"

- In John 13:18, Jesus referenced Psalm 41:9—"I do not speak concerning all of you. I know whom I have chosen; but that the Scripture may be fulfilled, 'He who eats bread with Me has lifted up his heel against Me.'"

The difficulty with the resurrection is the New Testament does not quote any Old Testament verse identifying the prophecy that it would take place on the third day. Is it possible there is no such prophecy? No:

- In Luke 24:46, Jesus said, "*Thus it is written*, and thus it was necessary for the Christ to suffer and to *rise from the dead the third day.*"
- In 1 Corinthians 15:4, Paul said, "[Jesus] was buried, and that He rose again *the third day according to the Scriptures.*"

Jesus said, "It is written" in the Old Testament that He would "rise [on] the third day." Paul said "the Scriptures" prophesied, not just that Jesus would be raised, but on "the third day." Where is this prophecy? There are three possibilities.

Jonah

The Book of Jonah was written about 760 BC. Almost eight centuries before Jesus was born, Jonah served as an amazing "sign" of His death, burial, and resurrection.

When the religious leaders asked for a sign in Matthew 12:39–40, Jesus rebuked them saying:

> "An evil and adulterous generation seeks after a sign, and no sign will be given except the sign of the prophet Jonah. For as Jonah was three days and three nights in the belly of the great fish, so will the Son of Man be three days and three nights in the heart of the earth."

Jesus said Jonah served as a "sign" of His death, burial, and resurrection. Jonah 1:17 says: "The Lord had prepared a great fish to swallow Jonah. And Jonah was in the belly of the fish three days and three nights."

The language takes our minds to the New Testament where the same words are used of Christ. Jonah "died" when the fish swallowed him. He was "buried" while in the fish. The imagery in the verses is so strong you could almost wonder if Jonah is alive or dead. For example, Jonah 2:2 records:

> And he said: "I cried out to the LORD because of my affliction, and He answered me. *Out of the belly of Sheol I cried,* and You heard my voice."

We would expect Jonah to say, "Out of the belly of *the fish* I cried," but he said he was in Sheol. Sheol is not heaven or hell. Instead, it is the temporary abode of the dead until people are resurrected to their eternal homes in heaven or hell. The Greek New Testament parallel is Hades, which makes the typology with Jesus very strong because Jesus was in Hades while He was buried: "[David] spoke concerning the resurrection of the Christ, that His soul was not left in Hades, nor did His flesh see corruption" (Acts 2:31). Continuing the burial imagery, Jonah 2:6 says:

"I went down to the moorings of the mountains;
The earth with its bars closed behind me forever;
Yet You have brought up my life from the pit,
O Lord, my God."

You would expect Jonah to say the water closed behind him, but instead, he says, "the earth." This is not the language of burial in the ocean. This is the language of burial in the ground. The pit is a synonym for Sheol and Hades, and Jonah expected to be "brought up," or raised, from the pit. He looked forward to his resurrection, just like Jesus looked forward to His resurrection! Jesus said, "You will not leave my soul in Hades, nor will You allow Your Holy One to see corruption" (Acts 2:27). Jonah's "resurrection" occurred in verse 10:

So the LORD spoke to the fish, and it vomited
Jonah onto dry land.

When Jonah came out of the fish, he probably felt like he came back from the dead and was given new life. Like Jesus, Jonah was "buried" for three days and three nights, and he might serve as a prophecy of Jesus' resurrection on the third day.

Hosea

Hosea 5:14–6:2 records the second likely prophecy of Jesus' resurrection on the third day. God speaks in Hosea 5:14–15:

> And like a young lion to the house of Judah.
> I, even I, will tear them and go away;
> I will take them away, and no one shall rescue.
> I will return again to My place
> Till they acknowledge their offense.
> Then they will seek My face;
> In their affliction they will earnestly seek Me."

These words sound harsh, but they serve the beautiful purpose of turning Israel back to God. The people respond in Hosea 6:1–2:

> Come, and let us return to the LORD;
> For He has torn, but He will heal us;
> He has stricken, but He will bind us up.
> After two days He will revive us;
> *On the third day He will raise us up,*
> That we may live in His sight.

The words about being "[raised] on the third day" take our minds to Christ. Although these verses discuss Israel, the complete fulfillment is in Jesus. He is the ideal Israel according to Isaiah 49:3:

And He said to me,
"You are My Servant, O Israel,
In Whom I will be glorified."

Israel is also called God's son:

- Exodus 4:22—"Then you shall say to Pharaoh, 'Thus says the Lord: "Israel is My son, My firstborn."'"
- Hosea 11:1—"When Israel was a child, I loved him, And out of Egypt I called My son."

The New Testament shows these verses about Israel serve as prophecies of Jesus. Matthew 2:14–15 quotes Hosea 11:1:

When he arose, he took the young Child and His mother by night and departed for Egypt, and was there until the death of Herod, that it might be fulfilled which was spoken by the Lord through the prophet, saying, "Out of Egypt I called My Son."

These verses about Israel look forward to Christ. That is also the case with Hosea 6:2, which goes beyond Israel's rebirth to Christ's resurrection. First Peter 1:10–11 loosely says, "all the prophets testified of the sufferings of Christ and the glory that should follow." They might not have been aware of the future reality of their words, but they are fulfilled in Christ. Regarding "He will raise us up," Adam Clarke said, "These words are supposed to refer to the

37

resurrection of our Lord. The original, *yekimenu*, has been translated, 'He will raise him up.'"[14] The words "may live in His sight" are like Isaiah 53:10, which says, "He shall prolong His days."

The context wonderfully supports Jesus being in view. The words, "I will tear… He has torn" look to Christ's body "torn" on the cross. When He died, "the veil of the temple was torn in two" (Matthew 27:51). Hebrews 10:20 says we have access to God "by a new and living way which He consecrated for us, through the veil, that is, His flesh." The veil was a picture of Christ's body that when "torn" gave us access to God. The words "He has stricken" point to Christ Who was "stricken, smitten by God, and afflicted" (Isaiah 53:4).

The words, "He will revive us… He will raise us up, that we may live in His sight," are a suitable prophecy because Jesus is the firstfruits of the resurrection (1 Corinthians 15:20–23). There is a close relationship between Jesus and His people, who are called "the body of Christ" (1 Corinthians 12:27). The resurrection of His body is their resurrection: "We shall be [united together with Him] in the likeness of His resurrection" (Romans 6:5).

Isaac

> Genesis 22:4—Then *on the third day* Abraham lifted his eyes and saw the place afar off.

Genesis 22 is one of the most unique types in the Old Testament because while others foreshadow Christ's death *or* resurrection, Abraham and Isaac foreshadow Christ's death *and* resurrection, with a confirmation in the New Testament:

- Hebrews 11:17 prefigures Christ's sacrifice through Isaac.
- Hebrews 11:19 prefigures Christ's resurrection through Isaac.

Genesis 22:4 is not only referring to the day Abraham arrived at Moriah. The verse also identifies the day Abraham received Isaac back from the dead. Hebrews 11:17 says:

By faith Abraham, when he was tested, *offered up* Isaac, and he who had received the promises *offered up* his *only begotten son*…

Twice it says Isaac was "offered up," drawing a parallel between him and Jesus Who was "offered up for our sins" (Romans 4:25). Second, Isaac is given the same title as Jesus: "only begotten son." Hebrews 11:18 says:

Of whom it was said, "In Isaac your seed shall be called"…

This quote from Genesis 21:12 identifies Isaac as the promised son Abraham's descendants would come from, as opposed to Ishmael. Hebrews 11:19 says:

Concluding that God was able to *raise him up, even from the dead*, from which he also received him in a figurative sense.

The words "raise him up, even from the dead," create the imagery that Isaac was resurrected. When Abraham received the command to sacrifice Isaac, he was so committed to obeying; it was as though Isaac died to him. This was the first day. Abraham reached Mount Moriah "on the third day." He ascended the mountain to sacrifice his son, and when the Angel of the LORD stopped him, it was as though he "received [Isaac]" back from the dead. This occurred "in a figurative sense," because Isaac did not physically die.

The Greek word for "figurative" is *parabolē*, which is related to our English word "parallel." It means, "a placing of one thing by the side of another, juxtaposition."[15] Of the fifty times the word occurs in the New Testament, forty-six times it is translated as "parable." Jesus' parables were physical stories placed alongside spiritual realities. The physical story of Abraham and Isaac illustrated the spiritual reality of Jesus' death and resurrection on the third day.

Isaac and Jesus Carried the Wood for Their Sacrifices

Genesis 22:6—So Abraham took the wood of the burnt offering and *laid it on Isaac his son*; and he took the fire in his hand, and a knife, and the two of them went together.

The wood for the burnt offering is emphasized throughout the account—mentioned five times in verses 3, 6, 7 and twice in verse 9. The wood looks to the cross. In both accounts, the wood was the physical instrument on which both Isaac and Jesus would be sacrificed. John 19:17 says, "[Jesus], bearing His cross, went out to a place called the Place of a Skull, which is called in Hebrew, Golgotha." Just like Jesus carried the wood for His sacrifice on His shoulders when He went to die, so did Isaac carry the wood for his sacrifice on his shoulders when he went to die.

Isaac and Jesus Were Willing to Experience Their Father's Fire

Genesis 22:6—So Abraham took the wood of the burnt offering and laid it on Isaac his son; and *he took the fire in his hand,* and a knife, and the two of them went together.

The fire is mentioned twice, in verses 6 and 7. We would expect verse 6 to say Abraham took the implements for building the fire, but instead, it says he "took the fire in his hand" (NKJV, ESV, NASB) or "carried the fire" (NIV). This sounds odd, but it looks forward to God's wrath, which is commonly associated with fire:

- Jeremiah 21:12 (ESV)—"Thus says the LORD: 'Execute justice in the morning, and deliver from the hand of the oppressor him who has been robbed, lest *my wrath go forth like fire*, and burn with none to quench it, because of your evil deeds.'"
- Ezekiel 22:31—"'I have poured out My indignation on them; I have consumed them with the *fire of My wrath*,'... says the Lord God."
- Zephaniah 1:18—"In the day of *the LORD's wrath*; but the whole land shall be devoured by the *fire of His jealousy*."

When God poured out His wrath on Sodom and Gomorrah, He rained fire and brimstone from heaven (Genesis 19:24, Luke 17:29). The location for unbelievers who experience God's wrath for eternity is "the lake of fire" (Revelation 19:20, 20:10, 14, 15). When Abraham carried the fire, it prefigured the wrath God the Father would pour out and the Son would consume. Jesus prayed, "O My Father, if it is possible, let this cup pass from Me; nevertheless, not as I will, but as You will" (Matthew 26:39).

Jesus drank the Father's wrath that believers deserve, so there is no more due us. Lamentations 3:22 says, "Through the LORD's mercies *we are not consumed*, because His compassions fail not." We are not consumed by God's wrath, because Jesus was willing to receive it for us. God's mercy doused the fire for Christians when He lit the fire for His Son.

Questions

1. Describe the similarities between Isaac and Jesus in Genesis 22:4–6.

2. Which parallel of Isaac and Jesus did you find to be most significant?

3. Why did Jesus (Luke 24:46) and Paul (1 Corinthians 15:4) say the Old Testament prophesied the resurrection would take place "on the third day"?

4. How does Jonah serve as a "sign" of Christ's death, burial, and resurrection?

5. What do the fire and wood represent?

6. Why were Isaac and Jesus both willing to be sacrificed?

Chapter 4

Genesis 22:7–10
Isaac and Jesus Were... Part III

Isaac and Jesus Were Sacrificial Lambs

Genesis 22:7–8—But Isaac spoke to Abraham his
father and said, "My father!"
And he said, "Here I am, my son."
Then he said, "Look, the fire and the wood, but
where is the lamb for a burnt offering?"
And Abraham said, "My son, *God will provide for
Himself the lamb* for a burnt offering." So the two of
them went together.

As already discussed in Chapter Three, Abraham
thought he would sacrifice Isaac, and then God
would raise him from the dead. Hebrews 11:19
says he "[concluded] that God was able to raise him up,

even from the dead." If Abraham expected to sacrifice Isaac, why did he also say God would provide a lamb? The best solution is Abraham saw Isaac as the lamb to be sacrificed.[16] This further establishes the typology between Isaac and Jesus.

When Isaac said, "Where is the lamb?" he asked one of the most important questions in history. When Abraham answered Isaac's question, he provided one of the most important answers in history. God would provide a lamb, and John the Baptist identified Him two thousand years later when he said, "Behold! The Lamb of God Who takes away the sin of the world" (John 1:29). This was when Isaac's question was finally answered, and Abraham's words were finally fulfilled.

Isaac and Jesus Were In Agreement with Their Father

Genesis 22:6, 8—So Abraham took the wood of the burnt offering and laid it on Isaac his son; and he took the fire in his hand, and a knife, and *the two of them went together*... And Abraham said, "My son, God will provide for Himself the lamb for a burnt offering." So *the two of them went together*.

The unity between father and son is shown through the repetition of, "the two of them went together." Consider these verses:

- John 3:16—"For God so loved the world that He gave His only begotten Son, that whoever believes in Him should not perish but have everlasting life."
- 1 John 3:16—"By this we know love, because He laid down His life for us."

The gospel makes us think of the Father's love for lost sinners (John 3:16), and the Son's love for those He died for (1 John 3:16), but this all required the Father and Son working together. Amos 3:3 asks, "Can two walk together, unless they are agreed?" The agreement between Abraham and Isaac pictures the agreement between God the Father and God the Son. In John 10:30 Jesus said, "I and My Father are one." In Jesus' high priestly prayer in John 17:21–23, He said:

> That they all may be one, *as You, Father, are in Me, and I in You*; that they also may be one in Us, that the world may believe that You sent Me. And the glory which You gave Me I have given them, that they may be one just *as We are one*: I in them, and *You in Me*.

Acts 20:28 says, "The church of God which He purchased with His own blood." We would expect the verse to say, "The church of God which Jesus purchased with His blood," or "The church of God which He purchased with His Son's blood." The mention of God purchasing the church with His own blood identifies Jesus as God. If Jesus shed His blood and God purchased the church with "His own blood," then Jesus must be God. John 3:16 says, "God so loved the world that He gave His only begotten Son." The Father and Son cooperated, and this was prefigured two thousand years earlier when Abraham and Isaac walked to Mount Moriah together.

Isaac and Jesus Were
Submissive to Their Fathers

Genesis 22:9—Then they came to the place of which God had told him. And Abraham built an altar there and placed the wood in order; and *he bound Isaac his son* and laid him on the altar, upon the wood.

The summer after eighth grade, I flew from California to upstate New York to work on my uncle's dairy farm. Being thirteen years old and having no friends in the area, I had to find things to do to entertain myself. A bull stood at the end of the barn staring straight ahead all day. Once, I decided it would be fun to try to get him to move. Since he did not enjoy this as much as I did, he brought his head up underneath me and launched me into the air. Think of a cowboy thrown off a bull during a rodeo, and you have the correct imagery. Fortunately, the barn's ceiling was high, so I did not slam into it, but I did come crashing down onto the cement floor.

One man who worked on the farm saw what happened and ran down to me. He screamed, "You could have gotten yourself killed! Do you see that little chain around the bull's neck? That is all that is holding him there, and he could break it at any moment!"

My first thought was, "They need to put a bigger chain around his neck!" My second thought was, "That bull has so much strength, but he allows himself to be subdued by so little." Unfortunately, we think of submission as a sign of weakness, but it is much like the bull—strength that is kept under control. Submission is a choice; it is deliberate and willful. Submission that is forced is not submission.

To appreciate Isaac's submission, we must dispel the incorrect images of Abraham sacrificing a small boy who was helpless against his stronger, more powerful father. Genesis 22:5 says, "And Abraham said to his young men, 'Stay here with the donkey; the lad and I will go yonder and worship, and we will come back to you.'" The Hebrew word for "young men" and "lad" is *na'ar*.[17] Even though Abraham called Isaac "lad," we should not think he was younger than the servants. The amount of wood needed to build the altar was significant, and Isaac was strong enough to carry it to the top of the mountain, even though it was "afar off" (Genesis 22:4).

Sarah had Isaac when she was ninety (Genesis 17:17). Genesis 23:1 says she died when she was one hundred twenty-seven years old. Isaac was thirty-seven at that time, which makes him somewhat younger in Genesis 22. Considering the account is a picture of what God would do with His Son two thousand years later, Isaac and Jesus could have been close in age when sacrificed.

Abraham was one hundred years old when Isaac was born, so add Isaac's age in Genesis 22 to one hundred and you get Abraham's age when he was going to sacrifice Isaac. Regardless of their exact ages, there was a strong, healthy son, and an old father. Isaac could have overpowered Abraham, but he kept his strength under control. Isaac's submission is the reason Abraham could "[bind] his son."

Why was Isaac submissive to Abraham? The simple, yet beautiful, answer is he trusted his father. The same was true with Jesus. First Peter 2:23 says, "When He was reviled, did not revile in return; when he suffered, He did not threaten, but *committed Himself to Him who judges righteously.*" Just like Isaac put his life in his father's hands, Jesus put His life in His Father's hands.

Nobody took Isaac's life from him, like nobody took Jesus' life from Him. Isaac's willingness to lay down his life pictures Jesus' willingness to lay down His life:

> "I am the good shepherd. The good shepherd *gives His life* for the sheep… As the Father knows Me, even so I know the Father; and *I lay down My life* for the sheep… And other sheep I have which are not of this fold; them also I must bring, and they will hear My voice; and there will be one flock and one shepherd… Therefore My Father loves Me, because *I lay down My life* that I may take it again. *No one takes it from Me, but I lay it down of Myself. I have power to lay it down*, and I have power to take it again.

This command I have received from My Father…
Greater love has no one than this, than to *lay down
one's life for his friends*." (John 10:11, 15, 17–18, 15:13)

First John 3:16 says, "By this we know love, because *He
laid down His life for us*." When the mob came to arrest Jesus,
Peter took out his sword to defend Him, and in Matthew
26:52–53, Jesus said, "Put your sword [away]… Do you
think that I cannot now pray to My Father, and He will
provide Me with more than twelve legions of angels?"
Jesus kept His authority and power under control. The
greater the restraint, the greater the submission. Since
nobody has ever had the power and authority of Jesus,
there has never been a greater demonstration of
submission than His. Isaac's submission is impressive, but
it pales in comparison to Jesus' submission. When we think
of Jesus' submission, we should think about:

- How He was willing to submit—perfectly
- What He was willing to submit to—the wrath of
  God our sins deserve
- Why He was willing to submit—His great love for
  us

Isaac and Jesus Were Placed
on the Wood for Their Sacrifices

Genesis 22:9—Then they came to the place of which
God had told him. And Abraham built an altar there

and placed the wood in order; and he bound Isaac his son and *laid him on the altar, upon the wood.*

When our first child, Rhea, was born, a doctor and some friends gave my wife, Katie, and me the same warning: "Do not cut your baby's nails with clippers. You could end up catching a finger." One time Katie used clippers, and sure enough, she cut Rhea's finger. Rhea was hurt, but Katie hurt even more. She felt so bad that she could not even talk about it without crying.

The injury was not serious. Our children have experienced much worse since then, but nothing has ever upset Katie as much. Why was she so troubled when she clipped Rhea's finger? Reflecting on the situation, I came to understand Katie was devastated because she caused Rhea's pain.

How must Abraham have felt when he laid Isaac on the wood and thought about what he would do? Just as much as Katie wished she could have been the one with the bleeding finger, Abraham must have wished he could be the one on the altar versus being the one standing beside it. Being able to take Isaac's place would have seemed too good to be true for this old man. In the years I have been a father, I have thought of this story and wondered if I could do what God called Abraham to do.

I do not know if I could have even watched Abraham do this. Seeing him bind his son would be almost unbearable. But in being placed on the wood, Isaac looks like Jesus Who was placed on the cross. Isaac did not climb on the wood any more than Jesus climbed on the cross. Imagine what this was like for Abraham with Isaac. Then imagine what it was like for God with His Son.

Isaac and Jesus Were Sacrificed by Their Father

Genesis 22:10—And Abraham stretched out his hand and *took the knife to slay his son.*

Abraham appears in control as he goes about the preparations. He rose early in the morning, saddled his donkey, took two servants with him, split the wood, departed, commanded the servants to remain behind, and placed the wood on his son. But never does Abraham look more sovereign over the sacrifice of his son than when he "took the knife to slay" him.

The knife is mentioned in verses 6 and 10, and it speaks of execution. Priests used knives for centuries to sacrifice animals, and Abraham would use one on Isaac. As responsible as Abraham would have been, had he sacrificed Isaac, God is that responsible for sacrificing Jesus. We say, "The Jews murdered their Messiah," or "The Romans crucified Jesus," or "Our sins nailed the Son of God to the cross." While these statements are true in that Jesus died for our sins, it is even truer to say the One Person responsible for crucifying Him was His Father.

When Pilate had Jesus before him, he mistakenly thought he had authority over Him. John 19:10–11 records:

> Then Pilate said to Him, "Are You not speaking to me? Do You not know that I have power to crucify You, and power to release You?"
> Jesus answered, "You could have no power at all against Me unless it had been given you from above."

Jesus let Pilate know the authority he had was given to him by God to accomplish His purpose. The only reason Pilate could do anything with Jesus was because Pilate's actions furthered God's plan for Christ to be crucified. Luke 22:22 says, "Truly the Son of Man goes as it has been determined [by God]." Acts 2:23 says Jesus was, "delivered by the determined purpose and foreknowledge of God." When the Christians in the early church prayed for boldness, Acts 4:27–28 records them saying:

> For truly against Your holy Servant Jesus, Whom You anointed, both Herod and Pontius Pilate, with the Gentiles and the people of Israel, were gathered together to do whatever Your hand and Your purpose determined before to be done.

At first, it sounds as though Christ's sacrifice is attributed to these individuals, but the final words declare it was God. All these people gathered together to see Christ crucified, but in doing so, they fulfilled God's predetermined plan. Herod, Pilate, the Gentiles, and the Jews could not have been more opposed to each other, but God banded them together to see Christ crucified.

Revelation 13:8 calls Jesus "the Lamb slain from the foundation of the world." The verse is in the past tense; how can it say Jesus was slain thousands of years before He was born in Bethlehem? This is called the Prophetic Perfect.[18] When God has determined something, it is so certain that it will take place that it is written as though it already happened. God the Father was so determined to sacrifice His Son for our sins that He wrote about it as though it had already taken place in the past.

Isaiah 53:10 also shows the Father responsible for the Son's sacrifice:

> It pleased the Lord to bruise Him;
> He has put Him to grief.
> When You make His soul an offering for sin…

The Lord "bruised Him… put Him to grief… made His soul an offering," and unbelievably, "it pleased the Lord" to do this. Elsewhere Scripture says God does not take pleasure in punishing the wicked:

- Ezekiel 18:23—"'Do I have any pleasure at all that the wicked should die?' says the Lord GOD, 'and not that he should turn from his ways and live?'"
- Ezekiel 33:11—"Say to them: 'As I live,' says the Lord GOD, 'I have no pleasure in the death of the

wicked, but that the wicked turn from his way and live. Turn, turn from your evil ways! For why should you die, O house of Israel?'"

God takes no pleasure in the death of the wicked, but He took pleasure in the death of His perfect, sinless Son? These verses are the opposite of what we would imagine. God was grieved, distraught, pained, and heartbroken are the words we would expect to read. How could God be pleased with His Son's death? Because of what it accomplished. Our redemption. Our forgiveness. Our righteousness. Our reconciliation. If the Father punished His Son, He would not have to punish us. If the Father poured out His wrath on Jesus, He would not have to pour out His wrath on us. God the Father sovereignly sacrificed His Son, and it was prefigured two thousand years earlier when Abraham walked up the mountain carrying the knife to sacrifice Isaac.

Isaac and Jesus Were Silent When Laying Down Their Lives

Genesis 22:10—And Abraham stretched out his hand and took the knife to slay his son.

Genesis 22:7 and 8 record a conversation between father and son:

But Isaac spoke to Abraham his father and said, "My father!"

And he said, "Here I am, my son."
Then he said, "Look, the fire and the wood, but
where is the lamb for a burnt offering?"
And Abraham said, "My son, God will provide for
Himself the lamb for a burnt offering." So the two
of them went together.

Isaac speaks to Abraham. He asks his father a question, and his father responds. Therefore, Isaac's silence before being sacrificed is astonishing. He is bound, laid on the altar, his father picks up the knife, but he does not say a word. Isaiah 53:7 prophesied of the same response from Jesus:

He opened not His mouth;
He was led as a lamb to the slaughter,
And as a sheep before its shearers is silent,
So He opened not His mouth.

The fulfillment was shown during Jesus' trials:

- Before Caiaphas, Matthew 26:62–63 records, "And the high priest arose and said to Him, 'Do You answer nothing? What is it these men testify against You?' But *Jesus kept silent.* And the high priest answered and said to Him, 'I put You under oath by the living God: Tell us if You are the Christ, the Son of God!'"
- Before Pilate, Matthew 27:12–14 records, "And while He was being accused by the chief priests and

elders, *He answered nothing.* Then Pilate said to Him, 'Do You not hear how many things they testify against You?' But *He answered him not one word,* so that the governor marveled greatly."

- Before Herod, Luke 23:9 records, "Then he questioned Him with many words, but *He answered him nothing.*"

Isaac's silence before his sacrifice prefigured Jesus' silence two thousand years later before His sacrifice.

Questions

1. Compare how the circumstances were the same for Isaac and Jesus in Genesis 22:7–10.

2. As you read the various similarities, did you think of any others? If so, what are they?

3. Aside from the crucifixion, how else did Jesus demonstrate agreement with His Father during His earthly life?

4. In what way(s) did Isaac and Jesus demonstrate submission?

5. What other demonstrations of submission in Scripture come to mind?

6. Why did it "please" God to put Jesus to death?

Chapter 5

Genesis 22:11–12
Together on Mount Moriah

To fully appreciate the greatness of what took place on Mount Moriah, we need a theology lesson.

Nobody Has Seen God the Father

Moses wanted to see God, but in Exodus 33:20 He said, "You cannot see My face; for no man shall see Me, and live." If people saw God, they would not live to talk about it! The New Testament confirms that nobody has seen God:

- 1 Timothy 6:16—"[God] Whom no man has seen or can see."
- 1 John 4:12—"No one has seen God at any time."

Hebrews 11:27 says, "By faith [Moses] forsook Egypt, not fearing the wrath of the king; for he endured as *seeing Him Who is invisible*." Moses "saw" God by faith because He could not see Him physically. Colossians 1:15 says God is "invisible." First Timothy 1:17 says, "The King eternal, immortal, *invisible*." The difficulty is that some people in the Old Testament did see God:

- When Jacob had his dream of the ladder that stretched between heaven and earth, he saw God standing at the top of it: "Behold, *the LORD stood above [the ladder]* and said: 'I am the LORD God of Abraham your father and the God of Isaac'" (Genesis 28:13).
- Moses and seventy-three elders saw God: "Then Moses went up, also Aaron, Nadab, and Abihu, and seventy of the elders of Israel, and *they saw the God of Israel*. And there was under His feet as it were a paved work of sapphire stone, and it was like the very heavens in its clarity" (Exodus 24:9–10).
- The prophet Micaiah told King Ahab, "*I saw the LORD sitting on His throne*, and all the host of heaven standing on His right hand and His left" (2 Chronicles 18:18).

How can it be explained that the New Testament says nobody has seen God, but the Old Testament records instances of people seeing God? The solution provides a better understanding of God's Word, the triune nature of God, and situations in Scripture that might seem odd, e.g.,

Jesus praying to God while being God. When Scripture says nobody has seen God, it means nobody has seen God the Father. Jesus said, "The Father Himself, Who sent Me, has testified of Me. You have neither heard His voice at any time, *nor seen His form*" (John 5:37) and "*Not that anyone has seen the Father*, except He Who is from God; He has seen the Father" (John 6:46).

Often when Scripture discusses God the Father, it simply says, "God." Consider these verses as examples:

- Romans 5:8—"God demonstrates His own love toward us in that while we were still sinners, Christ died for us." Paul is referring to God the Father.
- 1 Corinthians 11:3—"The head of Christ is God." Again, God the Father is in view.
- 1 John 4:9–10—"In this the love of God was manifested toward us, that God has sent His only begotten Son into the world, that we might live through Him. In this is love, not that we loved God, but that He loved us and sent His Son to be the propitiation for our sins."

In Matthew 27:46, Jesus prayed, "My God, My God, why have You forsaken Me?" People read this and ask, "How can Jesus *be* God and pray *to* God?" God exists as three distinct Persons, and God the Son is praying to God the Father. The reason Jesus did not call God "Father" as He did earlier throughout the gospels is because of the

63

separation taking place at that moment between Father and Son.

Similarly, even though Jesus is God, throughout the New Testament, He is often simply called "Jesus" or "Christ" or a combination of both titles to emphasize His messiahship. Other times He is called, "Son of God" to emphasize His deity, or "Son of Man" to emphasize His humanity. Despite what some false religions teach, identifying Jesus as the Son of God does not make Him less than God any more than identifying God as Father makes Him any less God. The religious leaders of Jesus' day understood that when Jesus called Himself the Son of God, He identified Himself as God. John 5:18 says, "Therefore the Jews sought all the more to kill Him, because He not only broke the Sabbath, but also *said that God was His Father, making Himself equal with God.*"

In the Old Testament, People Saw God the Son

If nobody has seen God the Father, who did Isaac, Moses, Aaron, Nadab, Abihu, the seventy elders of Israel, and Micaiah see when they saw God in the Old Testament? They saw the pre-incarnate Son of God. In Greek, "*theos*"[19] is "God," and "*phaino*"[20] is "appear," which is why Old Testament appearances of Jesus are known as Theophanies or Christophanies.[21] Considering that people saw God when they saw Jesus in the Old Testament is undeniable evidence that Jesus is God.

One of the most famous visions of God is in Isaiah 6, and the first verse says:

In the year that King Uzziah died, I saw the Lord sitting on a throne, high and lifted up, and the train of His robe filled the temple.

After witnessing this tremendous vision, in Isaiah 6:5 the prophet said:

"Woe is me, for I am undone! Because I am a man of unclean lips, and I dwell in the midst of a people of unclean lips; for *my eyes have seen the King, the LORD of Hosts.*"

Although it might be tempting to think Isaiah saw God the Father, since nobody has seen the first person of the Trinity, who did Isaiah see? He said he saw "the King, the Lord," and He did—Jesus Christ is the "King of Kings and Lord of Lords" (1 Timothy 6:15, Revelation 17:14, 19:16). The New Testament affirms this. Speaking of Isaiah 6, John 12:41 says, "Isaiah saw [Jesus'] glory and spoke of Him."

Another tremendous vision of God is in Ezekiel 1. Four angels carry the throne of God on a surface above their heads. Toward the end of the account, verse 26 says, "Above the firmament over their heads was the likeness of a throne [and on it] was a likeness *with the appearance of a man* high above it." This is the Son of God resembling a man before the Incarnation.

When Daniel's three friends were thrown into the fiery furnace, Daniel 3:24–25 says:

> Then King Nebuchadnezzar was astonished; and he rose in haste and spoke, saying to his counselors, "Did we not cast three men bound into the midst of the fire?"
> They answered and said to the king, "True, O king."
> "Look!" he answered, "I see four men loose, walking in the midst of the fire; and they are not hurt, and *the form of the fourth is like the Son of God.*"

Nebuchadnezzar saw the pre-incarnate Jesus Christ. John 1:18 provides a summary: "No one has seen God (the Father) at any time. The only begotten Son, Who is in the bosom of the Father, He (the Son) has declared Him (the Father)."

The NIV says the "Son, Who is Himself God… has made Him (the Father) known." God the Father is invisible, but God the Son revealed Him through these Old Testament appearances. Jesus is "the image of the invisible God" (Colossians 1:15 and 2 Corinthians 4:4) and "the brightness of [God's] glory and the express image of His person" (Hebrews 1:3). In John 12:45, Jesus said, "He who sees Me sees Him Who sent Me" referring to the Father. When Philip said, "Show us the Father," Jesus replied, "He who has seen Me has seen the Father; so how can you say, 'Show us the Father'?" (John 14:8–9).

The Angel of the Lord is God the Son

Unfortunately, sometimes people wrongly think Jesus "began" when He was born in Bethlehem; therefore, they do not recognize Him in the Old Testament. John 1:1 says: "In the beginning was the Word, and the Word was with God, and the Word was God." The Word is another name for Jesus. The verse distinguishes between the Word (Jesus) and God, while also identifying the Word (Jesus) as God. Jesus eternally existed with God and as God before becoming a Man. He was active throughout the Old Testament as the Angel of the LORD, who identifies Himself as God and acts as God.[22]

When God spoke to Moses through the burning bush, Exodus 3:2 says, "And the Angel of the LORD appeared to him in a flame of fire from the midst of a bush. So he looked, and behold, the bush was burning with fire, but the bush was not consumed." Then the Angel of the LORD is shown to be God. Exodus 3:4–6 records:

> So when the LORD saw that he turned aside to look, God called to him from the midst of the bush and said, "Moses, Moses!"
> And he said, "Here I am."
> Then He said, "Do not draw near this place. Take your sandals off your feet, for the place where you stand is holy ground." Moreover He said, *"I am the God of your father*—the God of Abraham, the God of

Isaac, and the God of Jacob." And Moses hid his face, for he was afraid to look upon God.

The Angel of the LORD spoke with Samson's parents and then disappeared. Judges 13:21–22 records:

When the Angel of the LORD appeared no more to Manoah and his wife, then Manoah knew that He was the Angel of the LORD. And Manoah said to his wife, "We shall surely die, because *we have seen God!*"

Manoah knew the Angel was God, and he knew God told Moses in Exodus 33:20: "No man shall see Me and live." What Manoah did not know was that Exodus 33:20 referred to God the Father, and the Angel he saw was God the Son. The Angel of the LORD appeared throughout the Old Testament, but He seems absent from the New Testament. He is present, but He became a Man: "The Word became flesh and dwelt among us" (John 1:14). The Angel of the LORD served God throughout the Old Testament and continued that ministry as a Man in the New Testament:

- John 5:30 and 6:38—Jesus said, "I do not seek My own will but the will of the Father Who sent Me."
- Matthew 26:39—"[Jesus] went a little farther and fell on His face, and prayed, saying, 'O My Father, if it is possible, let this cup pass from Me; nevertheless, not as I will, but as You will.'"

In John 4:34, Jesus said, "My food is to do the will of Him Who sent Me, and to finish His work." The Son of God became a Man to finish the work He started as the Angel of the LORD.

Throughout the Old Testament, God the Father prepared people to know His Son through these appearances. The Angel of the LORD foreshadowed the incarnation when God the Son would fully and permanently become a Man in the person of Jesus Christ.

The Intersection on Mount Moriah

With this foundation in mind, we can look at some verses, and I confess I feel inadequate to do them justice. Up to this point, we have discussed the ways Isaac is a type of Jesus, but with these verses, Jesus appears in the account as the Angel of the LORD. We have been dealing with types and shadows, but now the Substance and Reality arrives. Genesis 22:11–12 records:

> But the Angel of the LORD called to [Abraham]
> from heaven and said, "Abraham, Abraham!"
> So he said, "Here I am."
> And He said, "Do not lay your hand on the lad, or
> do anything to him; for now I know that you fear
> God, since you have not withheld your son, your
> only son, from Me."

The unique way the Angel of the LORD speaks sounds confusing. We would expect Him to say, "I know you fear God, since you did not withhold your son [from Him]" or "I know you fear [Me], since you have not withheld your son from Me." The Angel refers to God while also identifying Himself as God. The Angel is God but also separate from God. This only makes sense when considering God exists as three distinct persons.

Jesus intervened at this moment to prevent Isaac's sacrifice. He stopped Abraham a short distance from the location where He would be crucified two thousand years later. Isaac lay on the altar when the voice of the person he prefigured called out from heaven. Abraham and Isaac heard from the individual who would later die for their sins, fulfilling what they were only prefiguring.

Stopping the True and Greater Plague

When the Angel of the LORD stopped Abraham, this was the first of three times the pre-incarnate Christ appeared at this location on Mount Moriah. The second instance took place one thousand years later when David numbered the people. In Exodus 30:12, God commanded, "When you take the census of the children of Israel… then every man shall give a ransom… to the LORD… that there may be no plague." David numbered the people but did not give the ransom, and his actions brought a plague on the people. Part of 1 Chronicles 21:14–26 records:

So the LORD sent a plague upon Israel, and seventy thousand men of Israel fell… And *the Angel of the LORD stood by* the threshing floor of Araunah the Jebusite… The Angel of the LORD commanded [David to] erect an altar to the LORD on the threshing floor of Araunah the Jebusite… Then David said to Araunah, "Grant me the place of this threshing floor, that I may build an altar on it to the Lord, *that the plague may be withdrawn from the people.*" … And David built there an altar to the LORD, and offered burnt offerings and peace offerings, and called on the LORD; and *He answered him from heaven by fire* on the altar of burnt offering.

After David offered his sacrifice, God "answered him from heaven by fire." There are only three other instances of this happening in Scripture:

- After the priests were consecrated for worship and ready to offer sacrifices, Leviticus 9:24 says, "Fire came out from before the LORD and consumed the burnt offering and the fat on the altar."
- When Solomon dedicated the temple, 2 Chronicles 7:1 says, "Fire came down from heaven and consumed the burnt offering and sacrifices; and the glory of the Lord filled the temple."
- When Elijah was on Mt. Carmel facing hundreds of false prophets of Baal, 1 Kings 18:38 says, "Fire of the LORD fell and consumed the burnt sacrifice, and

the wood and the stones and the dust, and it licked up the water that was in the trench."

In each situation, something dramatic took place—the priesthood was established, the temple was dedicated, and Baal worship was removed. What was so significant about David's sacrifice that God would "answer from heaven by fire"? The timing and the location! Regarding the timing, David's sacrifice coincided with the plague ceasing and the turning away of God's wrath. After God answered from heaven by fire, 1 Chronicles 21:27 records, "So the LORD commanded the Angel, and He returned His sword to its sheath."

Regarding the location, this is where the temple would be built: "Solomon [built] the house of the LORD in Jerusalem *on Mount Moriah*, where the LORD had appeared to David his father… *on the threshing floor of Araunah the Jebusite*" (2 Chronicles 3:1). Wheat and chaff are separated on threshing floors, making them fitting pictures of judgment and an appropriate place for the temple. David's sacrifice was the first of many at this location.

Araunah's threshing floor was on Mount Moriah, which means this is also where God sent Abraham to sacrifice Isaac. The Angel of the LORD, the pre-incarnate Jesus Christ, first showed up at this location to stop Abraham from sacrificing Isaac. One thousand years later, at this same location, God the Father stopped the plague that threatened Jerusalem and the Angel of the LORD sheathed His mighty sword in response to David's repentant worship. Finally, going forward another one thousand years, at this same location, the Angel of the LORD stopped the true and greater plague that threatened all mankind when He was willing to hang on a cross.

David did not pay the ransom, and his sin brought a plague that affected one group of people for one moment in time. Adam sinned, but it brought a plague that affects every person throughout history: "Sin entered the world, and death through sin, and thus death spread to all men" (Romans 5:12). David offered burnt offerings and peace offerings following the plague in his day. What ransom is required to turn away the plague Adam brought on by his sin? Mark 10:45 says, "The Son of Man [gave] His life a ransom for many." Jesus stopped the true and greater plague, and His sinless, perfect life was the required payment.

Questions

1. Exodus 33:20, 1 Timothy 6:16, and 1 John 4:12 state no man has seen God. How can these verses be reconciled with Old Testament verses, such as Genesis 28:13 and 2 Chronicles 18:28 that discuss men seeing God?

2. What is a theophany or Christophany?

3. What verses teach that Jesus is God?

4. What are some examples of theophanies or Christophanies in the Old Testament that were not discussed in the chapter?

5. Why is Mount Moriah so significant?

6. How is the plague Jesus stopped worse than the plague in David's day?

Chapter 6

Genesis 22:13–19
Substitutions,
Seeds, and Brides

Substitutionary Atonement Revealed

Genesis 22:13–14—Then Abraham lifted his eyes
and looked, and there behind him was a ram caught
in a thicket by its horns. So Abraham went and took
the ram, and *offered it up for a burnt offering instead of his
son.* And Abraham called the name of the place, The-
LORD-Will-Provide; as it is said to this day, "In the
Mount of the LORD it shall be provided."

Isaac asked, "Where is the lamb?" and Abraham
answered, "God will provide a lamb" (Genesis 22:7–8).
The ram they found was not the lamb:

- The Hebrew word for "lamb" in verses 7 and 8 is *seh*, and it means, "one of a flock, lamb, sheep, goat."[23]
- The Hebrew word for "ram" in verse 13 is *avil*, and it means, "ram."[24]

Rams were used as sacrifices. The trespass (or guilt) offering was a mandatory sacrifice, and it was exclusively a ram (Leviticus 6:6). These offerings were given as atonement for unintentional sins that required reimbursing an offended party, and to cleanse from defiling sins and physical maladies. The fat, kidneys, and liver were offered to God, and the remainder of the ram had to be eaten inside the court of the tabernacle. On the Day of Atonement (Yom Kippur), a ram was sacrificed as a burnt offering (Leviticus 16:3–5).

Rams could also serve as burnt offerings, which is what God called for in Genesis 22:2.[25] Since rams could serve as burnt offerings, Abraham could offer this one "caught in [the] thicket...instead of his son." This is the language of substitutionary atonement that found its true and greatest fulfillment in Jesus. Consider the language in Isaiah 53:5–12:

> He was wounded for our transgressions,
> He was bruised for our iniquities;
> The chastisement for our peace was upon Him...
> The LORD has laid on Him the iniquity of us all...
> For [our] transgressions He was stricken...

The [LORD made] His soul an offering for sin…
He shall bear their iniquities…
He bore the sin of many…

The ram died in Isaac's place, looking forward to Jesus dying in our place. The ram rescued Isaac from physical death, just as Jesus rescues believers from spiritual death.

Why did God provide a ram instead of a lamb that would have better prefigured Jesus, the Lamb of God? By providing a ram, there is no doubt that Abraham's words were not fulfilled; it is obvious a lamb was still required.

In Hebrew, "The-LORD-Will-Provide" is "Jehovah Jireh."[26] In verse 8, Abraham said, "My son, God will provide for Himself the lamb for a burnt offering." If Abraham saw the ram as the sacrifice God would provide, he would have called the place, "The LORD Has Provided." Instead, Abraham called it "The-LORD-Will-Provide," because he looked forward to a future day when God would provide the required lamb.

There is evidence Abraham passed along his revelation to subsequent generations. The words "as it is said to this day" (Genesis 22:14) refer to the day Moses wrote Genesis; therefore, five centuries later, people were still saying, "it shall be provided." The words "In the Mount of the LORD," mean they looked forward to God providing at this location on Mount Moriah.

Unlike people in the Old Testament, we can say, "The LORD has provided!" We can proclaim with great joy and thanksgiving that the Lamb Who takes away the sins of the world was offered up as our Substitute.

Abraham Saw Jesus through Isaac

We see Jesus through Isaac, but did Abraham? Could he have had any idea he was prefiguring what God the Father would do with His Son two thousand years later? Could he know the Angel Who stopped him from sacrificing his son was the Person his son represented and the Person Who would later die for them both?

In John 8:56, Jesus said, "Abraham rejoiced to see My day, *and he saw it and was glad.*" Saying Abraham rejoiced to see Christ's day means nothing more than he looked forward to the fulfillment of the promises God made him. Jesus went beyond that, though, in saying Abraham did see His day! Abraham saw Jesus—including His sacrifice— through Isaac. He had at least a veiled, shadowy idea of the true and greater reality taking place:

- Warren Wiersbe said, "When Isaac willingly [allowed himself to be] put on the altar, Abraham saw the day of Christ's death and resurrection."[27]
- A.W. Pink said, "How did Abraham 'see' Christ's day? Abraham saw the day of Christ in type. In offering Isaac on the altar and in receiving him back in a figurative sense from the dead [as Hebrews 11:19 says], he received a marvelous foreshadowing of the Savior's death and resurrection."[28]

- *The Moody Bible Commentary* says, "Abraham witnessed through the binding of Isaac a foreshadowing of the death and resurrection of Christ."[29]
- Albert Barnes said, "Abraham was permitted to have a view of the death of the Messiah as a sacrifice for sin, represented by the command to offer Isaac."[30]
- Matthew Poole said, "[Abraham] saw [Christ's day] in the type of Isaac being offered, then receiving him [back]."[31]
- John Gill said, "He saw Christ and his day, his sufferings, death, and resurrection from the dead, in a figure; in the binding of Isaac, in the sacrifice of the ram, and in the receiving of Isaac [back] from the dead."[32]

Consider these two verses:

- Psalm 25:14—"The secret of the LORD is with those who fear Him, and He will show them His covenant."
- Hebrews 9:15—[Jesus is] "the Mediator of the new covenant, by means of death."

Abraham feared God, and God showed him the New Covenant by revealing the Mediator of the covenant through Isaac. Romans 4:11 says Abraham is "the father of all those who believe." Even though Abraham was in the Old Testament, he is able to be the father of New Covenant believers because God revealed His Son to him, and he looked forward to that Son in faith. Thus, people in the Old Testament were saved by grace through faith in the same way we are saved in the New Testament—by grace through faith. They looked forward in faith, while we look back in faith.

The Seed of Abraham

> Genesis 22:17–18—"Blessing I will bless you, and multiplying I will multiply your descendants as the stars of the heaven and as the sand which is on the seashore; and your descendants shall possess the gate of their enemies. *In your seed all the nations of the earth shall be blessed*, because you have obeyed My voice."

Abraham's seed is Isaac, but God's words look past him to Jesus, the true and greater "Son of Abraham" (Matthew 1:1). The previous verses in Genesis 22 have been filled with typology, but with these verses, a direct connection is made to Jesus. Peter identified Jesus as the Seed when he quoted Genesis 22:18 while preaching in Acts 3:25–26:

> You are sons of the prophets, and of the covenant which God made with our fathers, saying to Abraham, "And in your seed all the families of the earth shall be blessed." To you first, God, having raised up His Servant Jesus, sent Him to bless you,

in turning away every one of you from your iniquities.

Paul also referred to Jesus when he quoted Genesis 22:18 in Galatians 3:8:

And the Scripture, foreseeing that God would justify the Gentiles by faith, preached the gospel to Abraham beforehand, saying, "In you all the nations shall be blessed."

Unfortunately, some people think the gospel is a New Testament invention, but Paul says God preached the gospel to Abraham. The words, "In you all the nations shall be blessed" do not sound like a gospel presentation to us because there is no mention of Jesus' name, death, burial, or resurrection, but God's promise allowed Abraham to be saved by grace when he looked forward in faith to the Seed that would bless all nations. Genesis 15:6 says Abraham "believed in the Lord, and He accounted it to him for righteousness." Paul identified Jesus as the Seed in Galatians 3:16:

Now to Abraham and his Seed were the promises made. He does not say, "And to seeds," as of many, but as of one, "And to your Seed," Who is Christ.

Although God promised Abraham countless descendants, He spoke of one specific Seed "Who is Christ." All the descendants of Abraham—Moses, David,

Solomon, Isaiah, or any others—pale in comparison to Jesus because only through Him would "all the nations of the earth be blessed." Abraham spent years looking forward in faith to the birth of his son, Isaac, but Jesus is the only Son he could look forward to in faith for salvation.

Isaac and Jesus Return with Their Brides

Genesis 22:19—"So *Abraham returned to his young men,* and they rose and went together to Beersheba; and Abraham dwelt at Beersheba."

As already discussed, Genesis 22 prefigures Jesus' death and resurrection, but it also prefigures His return with His bride, the church. Verse 19 says "Abraham returned to his young men," but where is Isaac? When Abraham left the two servants, he said, "Stay here with the donkey; the lad and I will go yonder and worship, and *we will come back to you*" (Genesis 22:5). Previously, verses 6 and 8 say, "The two of them went together." Why did they not return together?

This furthers Isaac's typology with Jesus Who "disappeared" after the Ascension until He returns with His Bride, the church. Similarly, Isaac is "sacrificed," "resurrected," and then he disappears. We do not see him again until he returns with his bride, Rebekah.

Abraham maintains the typology with God the Father by sending out a servant to find a bride for his son. God the Father sent out a Servant—the Holy Spirit—to find a bride for His Son. Genesis 24:2–4 records:

> So Abraham said to the oldest servant of his house, who ruled over all that he had, "Please, put your hand under my thigh, and I will make you swear by the LORD, the God of heaven and the God of the earth, that you will not take a wife for my son from the daughters of the Canaanites, among whom I dwell; but you shall go to my country and to my family, and take a wife for my son Isaac."

Based on Genesis 15:2, we know the servant's name is Eliezer, which means "God is help."[33] This makes the connection with the Holy Spirit Who is "the Helper" (John 14:16, 26, 16:7). Even though the servant's name is known, it is not mentioned anywhere in the account, furthering the typology with the Holy Spirit, Who is the Unnamed Servant working behind the scenes.

In Genesis 24:27, Isaac told Rebekah:

> "Blessed be the LORD God of my master Abraham, Who has not forsaken His mercy and His truth toward my master. As for me, being on the way, the LORD led me to the house of my master's brethren."

Rebekah was chosen for marriage before she knew it. As Christ's bride, we were chosen before we knew it: "He chose us in Him *before the foundation of the world*" (Ephesians

1:4). The servant gave Rebekah gifts. Genesis 24:53 says, "The servant brought out jewelry of silver, jewelry of gold, and clothing, and gave them to Rebekah." The Holy Spirit gives us gifts: "Each one has received a gift" (1 Peter 4:10).

Rebekah's brother, Laban, was a worldly man who tried to delay his sister from obeying the servant and going to her husband. Genesis 24:54–58 records:

> [The servant] said, "Send me away to my master [Isaac]."
> But [Laban and Rebekah's mother] said, "Let the young woman stay with us a few days, at least ten; after that she may go."
> And he said to them, "Do not hinder me, since the LORD has prospered my way; send me away so that I may go to my master."
> So they said, "We will call the young woman and ask her personally." Then they called Rebekah and said to her, "Will you go with this man?"
> And she said, "I will go."

While the Unnamed Servant seeks to bring us to Christ, the world—pictured by Laban—seeks to delay us. Rebekah heard about the wealthy father with a beloved son. She was invited to leave her old life and find a new life, and she did not hesitate to go to her bridegroom. She shows the obedience that should characterize the church in not hesitating to go to our Bridegroom. We know there is a wealthy Father with a beloved Son, and we are invited to leave our lives and begin new lives with Him. As Rebekah joyfully went to Isaac, we should joyfully leave the world for Christ.

Rebekah did not know Isaac. She learned of him through his representative. Similarly, we do not know Christ, but we learn of Him through the Holy Spirit. Rebekah had not seen Isaac, but she still desired him. We have not seen Jesus, but "Whom having not seen [we] love" (1 Peter 1:8).

Rebekah was entrusted to the servant until she met her bridegroom. Genesis 24:61 says, "Then Rebekah and her maids arose, and they rode on the camels and followed the man. So the servant took Rebekah and departed." Similarly, the church is entrusted to the Holy Spirit until we meet our Bridegroom. Genesis 24:64–65 records Isaac and Rebekah's meeting:

> Then Rebekah lifted her eyes, and when she saw
> Isaac she dismounted from her camel; for she had
> said to the servant, "Who is this man walking in the
> field to meet us?"
> The servant said, "It is my master." So she took a
> veil and covered herself.

Rebekah's long journey to Isaac was finally over. There will be a day when our long journey to Christ will finally be over. Isaiah 25:9 says:

> And it will be said in that day: "Behold, this is our
> God; we have waited for Him, and He will save us.

> This is the LORD; we have waited for Him; we will
> be glad and rejoice in His salvation."

The Type Never Lives up to the Reality

We have considered many wonderful ways Abraham and Isaac are great types of God the Father and God the Son, but types always come up short. Types are "shadow(s) of things to come, but the substance is of Christ" (Colossians 2:17). Types are not "the true form of these realities." If types did not fall short, they would not be types. They would have the substance and be the reality. This is the case with Abraham and Isaac. Genesis 22 contains one of the most amazing types in Scripture, but it breaks down.

Abraham was with Isaac the whole time. The intimacy between them is shown when they speak to each other. Isaac called Abraham, "My father" and Abraham called Isaac, "My son" (Genesis 22:7). There was no intimacy between God the Father and God the Son when Jesus was sacrificed. Throughout the gospels Jesus called God, "My Father," but when He hung on the cross, the intimacy was broken. There was only separation. Jesus said, "My God, My God, why have You forsaken Me?" (Matthew 27:46). Abraham carried the knife and fire, but Isaac was spared from both. Jesus, on the other hand, experienced the full weight of God's wrath.

God did not want Isaac sacrificed because it would have accomplished nothing. Sin would not have been transmitted. Atonement would not have been made. It would not have pleased the Lord to bruise Isaac, like it "pleased the Lord to bruise" Jesus (Isaiah 53:10).

The question remains then, did God want a burnt offering? Yes, He did! He wanted our sins transmitted. He wanted atonement made. He chose His Son to be the sacrifice. If you have repented of your sins and put your faith in Christ, then "the LORD has laid on Him [your] iniquity" (Isaiah 53:6). If you have not done this, your sins remain on you.

God loves you and will forgive you, but John 3:16 says, "God so loved the world…" not, "The world so loved God." Many will reject Jesus, which is why in Matthew 7:13–14 He said:

> Enter by the narrow gate; for wide is the gate and broad is the way that leads to destruction, and there are *many who go in by it*. Because narrow is the gate and difficult is the way which leads to life, and there are few who find it.

The words "many" and "few" describe the number of people going to hell versus heaven. What percent do many and few represent—is it sixty-forty? Seventy-thirty? Maybe even eighty-twenty? The Lord does not tell us the percent, but He does tell us it is "many" versus "few," and that alone should create a healthy fear. When Jesus said "narrow," He meant narrow. There is only one way to be saved, and that is by grace through faith in Christ. In John 14:6, Jesus said, "I am the Way (singular), and the Truth, and the Life. No one comes to the Father except through Me." In Acts 4:12, the apostle Peter preached to the religious leaders: "Nor is there salvation in any other, for there is no other name under heaven given among men by which we must be saved." Only one way and one name. This is narrow, and there are "few" people who find this "narrow way which leads to life."

My prayer is that you have found "the way which leads to life." Second Corinthians 6:2 says "now is the day of salvation." Today you can embrace the Father's love for you. If you wonder if the Father really loves you, remember He gave "[His] Son, [His] only Son" Whom He loved for you (Genesis 22:2 cf. Matthew 3:17).

Questions

1. How was the ram a shadow of the greater reality fulfilled in Jesus?

2. Genesis 22:17–18 says, "In [Abraham's] seed all the nations of the earth shall be blessed." Where else in Scripture is this Seed mentioned?

3. In what ways does Isaac serve as a type of Christ *after* Abraham sacrificed the ram?

4. How does the typology break down between Isaac and Jesus? In other words, when does the type and shadow not match the reality and substance?

5. What verses would you quote to those who claim, "There are many ways to heaven"?

6. Think of one of the other types in Scripture. If you have trouble thinking of one, go back to the Introduction where a number are listed. How do these types fail to live up to the reality found in Christ?

Chapter 7

Learning from Abraham's Example

While we want to see Jesus throughout the account, we can also learn from Abraham's example. We can be encouraged by his great faith and challenged by his tremendous obedience.

Abraham was Ready to Obey God

Genesis 22:1—Now it came to pass after these things that God tested Abraham, and said to him, "Abraham!"
And he said, *"Here I am."*

If we asked why God would want Abraham to sacrifice his son, the other comparable question we would ask is: why was Abraham willing to sacrifice his son? The simple answer is he heard from God. Abraham's willingness to present Isaac as a burnt offering required he be fully convinced God had spoken to him. Otherwise, Abraham was insane at best, and evil at worst.

When God first spoke to Abraham, he responded with three words, which mean much more than, "I am here." They mean, "I am ready to serve You and do Your will!" Other godly men said these same words when they were willing to obey God. In each instance, God revealed His desire only *after* the person responded this way. For example:

- Jacob said these words in Genesis 46:2, and then God told him to head to Egypt.
- Moses said these words in Exodus 3:4, and then God sent him to deliver the Israelites.
- Samuel said these words in 1 Samuel 3:4, 5, 6, and 8, and then God revealed he would remove Eli's house.
- Isaiah said these words in Isaiah 6:8, and then God sent him as a prophet.

Abraham heard from God and responded appropriately. We should have the same responsive hearts toward God. Often, that is when God reveals His will for us. The Word of God is what we "hear." When we become convinced that God is speaking to us through Scripture, we are to respond as quickly and obediently as Abraham did.

Abraham Obeyed God
When It Did Not Make Sense

Genesis 22:2—Then He said, "Take now your son, *your only son* Isaac, whom you love, and go to the land of Moriah, and *offer him there as a burnt offering* on one of the mountains of which I shall tell you."

There are two reasons this was a difficult test for Abraham. First, and most obviously, it meant sacrificing his "only son whom he loved." Second, it seemed irrational. When God repeated His covenant to Abraham, He said, "Look now toward heaven, and count the stars if you are able to number them… So shall your descendants be" (Genesis 15:5; see also Genesis 12:2 and 17:6). Later, in Genesis 21:12, God said, "In Isaac your seed shall be called," letting him know the descendants would come from Isaac, as opposed to Ishmael.

When God commanded Abraham to sacrifice Isaac, Isaac had no children. The dilemma for Abraham was, "God promised me lots of descendants, and they are supposed to come through Isaac, but I have to sacrifice him before he has had any children?" Despite any confusion Abraham experienced, he obeyed.

God's Word might not always make sense, but we must still obey. In Isaiah 55:8–9, God says:

"For My thoughts are not your thoughts,
Nor are your ways My ways…

For as the heavens are higher than the earth,
So are My ways higher than your ways,
And My thoughts than your thoughts."

We will not always understand why God does what He does, and we will not always understand why God wants us to do what He wants us to do. Even at those times, we must trust Him and obey.

Abraham Did Not Delay Obeying

Genesis 22:3—So *Abraham rose early in the morning* and saddled his donkey, and took two of his young men with him, and Isaac his son; and he split the wood for the burnt offering, and arose and went to the place of which God had told him.

After receiving one of the most difficult commands given in Scripture, Abraham "rose early." He did not delay in doing what God wanted even though the thought of it must have been excruciating. He saddled his donkey and split the wood for the offering. Abraham had a large number of servants, and these are the tasks they would normally perform, but he did everything himself. More than likely he saw this as a command God gave to him alone.

The application is, delayed obedience is disobedience. When we know what God wants us to do, putting it off is the same as not doing it. James 4:17 says, "To him who knows to do good and does not do it, to him it is sin."

Abraham Would Not Let Anyone Interfere with Him Obeying

Genesis 22:5a—And Abraham said to his young men, *"Stay here with the donkey."*

There is no indication the servants knew what God told Abraham. More than likely they would try to restrain him from going through with the sacrifice when they learned what he had planned. We are not told whether it crossed his mind to allow them to go so they might stop him. When he arrived at the mount, he told his servants to stay behind, so they would not interfere.

We must not let anyone or anything interfere with us obeying God. While the servants would have thought they were preventing Abraham from making a terrible mistake, they would have been preventing him from obeying God. Sometimes it is well-meaning people who provide the greatest threat to us obeying. Matthew 16:21–23 records:

> From that time Jesus began to show to His
> disciples that He must go to Jerusalem, and suffer
> many things from the elders and chief priests and
> scribes, and be killed, and be raised the third day.
> Then Peter took Him aside and began to rebuke
> Him, saying, "Far be it from You, Lord; this shall

not happen to You!"
But He turned and said to Peter, "Get behind Me,
Satan! You are an offense to Me, for you are not
mindful of the things of God, but the things of
men."

Peter meant well, but Jesus would not let him interfere
with obeying His Father. Think of friends who say:

- "You shouldn't forgive your spouse because they'll
  just do it again!"
- "You might not have the money to buy that, but you
  deserve it after all you have been through!"
- "You will be in danger if you go to that part of the
  world as a missionary."

Sometimes obeying God means ensuring these people
do not interfere with us doing what God has called us to
do.

Abraham Understood Obedience Is Worship

Genesis 22:5b—The lad and *I will go yonder and
worship*, and we will come back to you.

The sacrifice God wants is obedience. King Saul did not
understand this, so Samuel rebuked him in 1 Samuel 15:22:

"Has the LORD as great delight in burnt offerings
and sacrifices, as in obeying the voice of the LORD?

Behold, to obey is better than sacrifice,
And to heed than the fat of rams."

God wants obedience more than He wants physical sacrifices. Proverbs 21:3 says, "To do righteousness and justice is more acceptable to the Lord than sacrifice." The Jews in Jeremiah's day were religious, but they were also disobedient. God rebuked them in Jeremiah 7:22–23 saying:

I did not… command them in the day that I brought them out of Egypt, concerning burnt offerings or sacrifices. But this is what I commanded them, saying, *"Obey My voice*, and I will be your God, and you shall be My people. And *walk in all the ways that I have commanded you*, that it may be well with you."

God said it was obedience, and not physical sacrifices, that would allow them to prosper. The greater the sacrifice involved in obeying God, the greater the worship; therefore, the greatest act of worship in the Old Testament might have taken place when Abraham was willing to sacrifice Isaac. We previously discussed The Principle of First Mention, and it is fitting the first use of the word "worship" occurs in Genesis 22:5.

Unfortunately, when some people hear "worship," they think of little more than singing in church. Abraham said sacrificing his son was worship because he understood worship takes place when we obey God.

And Abraham was not the only one "worshiping" on the mountain that day. He said Isaac would worship too because he saw Isaac's submission—something requiring immense obedience—as an act of worship too. The Apostle Paul wrote, "I appeal to you therefore, brothers, by the mercies of God, to *present your bodies as a living sacrifice*, holy and acceptable to God, which is *your spiritual worship*" (Romans 12:1 ESV). Second only to Christ, is there a better picture in Scripture of these words than Isaac?

We should live so obediently to God that our very lives are sacrifices. Complete surrender and submission is the greatest worship we can provide, and it does not take place on one day per week—it is a daily activity.

Abraham Trusted God

Genesis 22:5b—The lad and I will go yonder and worship, and *we will come back to you.*

How did Abraham resolve the seemingly impossible dilemma of God promising him children through Isaac, but then commanding him to sacrifice him? The answer is in Abraham's words to his servant: "We will come back." Abraham expected to sacrifice Isaac, and then return with him. He believed God would raise Isaac from the dead. Hebrews 11:19 says Abraham was "concluding that God was able to raise Isaac up, even from the dead." This answers the question of whether Abraham would have sacrificed Isaac. Yes, he would have, believing God would bring him back to life.

There are two reasons Abraham's faith is even greater than we might initially think. First, Abraham did not simply expect God to raise Isaac's intact body back from the dead. God commanded Abraham to offer Isaac as a burnt offering, which means he expected God to bring Isaac's body back from being turned into ashes.

Second, we are aware of God raising people from the dead: the widow of Zarephath's son (1 Kings 17:17–22), the Shunammite woman's son (2 Kings 4:32–35), Lazarus (John 11:1–44), and Dorcas (Acts 9:36–41) to name a few. Remembering these accounts makes it easier to believe in someone being raised from the dead. Abraham's faith is so great because there are no recorded instances of God raising anyone from the dead before Genesis 22. The idea that anyone could die and come back to life was completely novel. Abraham had to believe God would do something that there was no record of Him doing before.

Abraham knew there were only two possibilities. God would do something unprecedented, or He would become a liar. As impossible as it seemed to Abraham that God would raise Isaac from the dead, it seemed even more impossible that God would lie. Hebrews 6:18 says, "It is impossible for God to lie" and Abraham believed these words centuries before they were written.

As Abraham believed what God said to him, so must we believe what God says to us:

- As God's children, we are His heirs and joint heirs with Christ (Romans 8:17).
- God will never allow us to be tempted beyond what we are able to escape (1 Corinthians 10:13).
- We will receive glorified bodies (1 Corinthians 15:50–53).
- God's grace will be sufficient for the trials we experience (2 Corinthians 12:9).
- If we confess our sins, God is faithful and just to forgive us and cleanse us of all unrighteousness (1 John 1:9).

God's Sovereignty Should Give Us Confidence

I do not know what is going on in your life while you read this book, but if you have trouble trusting God or are worried about tomorrow, I hope you can find encouragement in Genesis 22. Two thousand years before Jesus' death, burial, and resurrection, Abraham and Isaac prefigured what God the Father had planned with His Son. This shows God's sovereignty—or control—over His Son's future. This should give us confidence in God's sovereignty over our futures.

When God spoke to Abraham, He knew what He would do in two thousand years, and He knew what He would do in your life. Should the Lord tarry, He knows what will happen next week, month, year, decade, century, millennium, and there is no thwarting His plans. He holds tomorrow in His hands, and He will cause "all things [to] work together for good to those who love [Him], to those who are the called according to His purpose" (Romans 8:28).

Questions

1. What most encouraged you about Abraham's example?

2. How can you apply Abraham's example of obedience to your life?

3. Who else in Scripture obeyed God in such a way their lives communicated, "I am ready to serve You and do Your will"?

4. Discuss a time you responded obediently to God's call on your life. What about a time you responded disobediently?

5. When obeying God does not make sense, how can you encourage yourself? What verses can you lean on?

6. How do you think God views delayed obedience?

7. Are there any ways people around you discourage your obedience to God? How can you respond to them?

8. How has your view of worship changed since reading about Abraham's worship in Genesis 22?

9. What promises of God do you most need to cling to, and why?

Chapter 8

The Wisdom of Fearing God

Genesis 22:12—And He said, "Do not lay your hand on the lad, or do anything to him; for *now I know that you fear God*, since you have not withheld your son, your only son, from Me."

The verse is not worded the way we would expect. Since God commanded Abraham to sacrifice "[his] only son, whom [he loved]," we would expect the Angel to say, "…now I know that you *love* God." Instead, the Angel focused on Abraham's *fear* of God. In John 14:15, Jesus said, "If you love Me, keep my commandments." Scripture teaches that love for God leads to obedience, but it also teaches that fear of God produces obedience, and an absence of fear of God creates disobedience. Pharaoh is a perfect example. Exodus 9:27–30 records:

And Pharaoh sent and called for Moses and Aaron, and said to them, "I have sinned this time. The LORD is righteous, and my people and I are wicked. Entreat the LORD, that there may be no more mighty thundering and hail, for it is enough. I will let you go, and you shall stay no longer."
So Moses said to him, "As soon as I have gone out of the city, I will spread out my hands to the LORD; the thunder will cease, and there will be no more hail, that you may know that the earth is the LORD's. But as for you and your servants, *I know that you will not yet fear the LORD God.*"

Moses said he would bring the seventh plague, hail, to an end, but he also knew Pharaoh would return to his old ways—he would repent of his repentance. As a result, three more plagues would follow. Pharaoh would continue to disobey because he did "not yet fear the LORD God."

Saul disobeyed when God told him to "utterly destroy [the Amalekites and] all that they have" (1 Samuel 15:3). He "spared Agag and the best of the sheep, the oxen, the fatlings, the lambs, and all that was good, and [was] unwilling to utterly destroy them. But everything despised and worthless, that they utterly destroyed" (1 Samuel 15:9). Saul was willing to destroy everything he did not want, but he kept what he wanted. God sent the prophet Samuel to rebuke Saul. First Samuel 15:24 records: "Then Saul said to Samuel, 'I have sinned, for I have transgressed the commandment of the LORD and your words, because *I feared the people and obeyed their voice.*" We obey the one we fear. Saul obeyed the people because he feared them more than God. Saul would have obeyed God if he feared God more than the people.

When the nation of Israel multiplied greatly in Egypt, Pharaoh became afraid of them. He commanded the Hebrew midwives: "When you... see [the Hebrew women] on the birthstools, if it is a son, then you shall kill him; but if it is a daughter, then she shall live" (Exodus 1:16). Unlike Saul, the Hebrew midwives feared God more than they feared man. Exodus 1:17 records, "The midwives feared God, and did not do as the king of Egypt commanded them, but saved the male children alive." Whatever we fear has power over us. If we fear God, we will obey God. If we fear man, we will obey man.

God brought Israel to the base of Sinai because His presence resided on the mountain. Considering everything He did to get them to this point—including delivering them from Egypt and parting the Red Sea—we would expect Him to be friendly and welcoming. Instead, Exodus 20:18–19 records:

> Now all the people witnessed the thunderings, the
> lightning flashes, the sound of the trumpet, and the
> mountain smoking; and when the people saw it,
> they trembled and stood afar off. Then they said to
> Moses, "You speak with us, and we will hear; but
> let not God speak with us, lest we die."

God put on a display that so terrified the Israelites they thought His voice would kill them. Moses explained God's motivation in Exodus 20:20:

> And Moses said to the people, "Do not fear; for God has come to test you, and that *His fear may be before you, so that you may not sin.*"

Moses told Israel their terror was good! Yes, God wanted to keep them away from the mountain so they would not be killed if they touched it, but He also wanted to build fear into them so they "may not sin." While Israel was at the base of Sinai, God also gave them the law. The law itself communicated that fear of God would prevent disobedience: "You shall not curse the deaf, nor put a stumbling block before the blind, but *shall fear your God*: I am the LORD" (Leviticus 19:14). If Israel feared God, they would obey in many ways such as treating people well.

After the twelve spies returned from scouting out the Promised Land, they led the nation to rebel against God. Ten of the spies convinced the people God wanted to murder them. Numbers 14:3 records the people's accusation: "Why has the LORD brought us to this land to fall by the sword, that our wives and children should become victims? Would it not be better for us to return to Egypt?" Here is part of God's response as verses 14:28–31 record:

> "As I live," says the LORD... "the carcasses of you who have complained against Me shall fall in this

wilderness, and all of you who were numbered, according to your entire number, from twenty years old and above… You shall by no means enter the land which I swore I would make you dwell in. But your little ones, whom you said would be victims, I will bring in, and they shall know the land which you have despised."

God caused Israel to wander so the adults who accused Him of murder could die in the wilderness. The children— whom the adults accused God of wanting to murder— could enter; however, they had not received the law as their parents had. Thus, God gave the law to the children too. This is recorded in Deuteronomy, which fittingly means, "Second Law."

When Moses gave the law to the new generation, he established the relationship between fear of God and obedience: "Therefore you shall keep the commandments of the LORD your God, *to walk in His ways and to fear Him*" (Deuteronomy 8:6). "Walking in God's ways" is synonymous with obedience, and it is produced by fearing Him. The psalmist said something similar: "Blessed is every one who *fears the LORD, who walks in His ways*" (Psalm 128:1). Fear of God and obedience to God go together. In Deuteronomy 31:12, Moses said, "Gather the people together, men and women and little ones, and the stranger who is within your gates, that they may hear and that they may learn to *fear the LORD your God and carefully observe all the words of this law.*" The entire nation had to be gathered so they would learn to fear God, because this would lead to their obedience. God made the same point through the prophets: "I will put *My fear in their hearts so that they will not depart from Me*" (Jeremiah 32:40).

While love might keep God's people near Him, fear keeps them from "[departing] from [Him]." In Jeremiah 2:19, God said Israel abandoned Him because they did not fear Him: "You have *forsaken the LORD your God*, and the *fear of Me is not in you.*" Like a protective wall, the fear of God keeps us close to Him.

Fear of God strengthened the early church: "Churches throughout all Judea, Galilee, and Samaria had peace *and were edified. And walking in the fear of the Lord* and in the comfort of the Holy Spirit, they were multiplied" (Acts 9:31). Paul commands us to pursue holiness because we fear God: "Beloved, let us cleanse ourselves from all filthiness of the flesh and spirit, *perfecting holiness in the fear of God*" (2 Corinthians 7:1). If we fear God, we will obey Him and that means purifying ourselves from whatever defiles us. Fear of God has a cleansing effect, producing holiness in us. Wickedness naturally becomes loathsome to those who fear God:

- Proverbs 8:13—"The fear of the LORD is to hate evil."
- Proverbs 16:6—"By the fear of the LORD one departs from evil" (see also Proverbs 3:7).

David Wilkerson said:

"What produces a consistent, lasting obedience? I am convinced that godly, loving obedience springs from one source: the fear of the living God! I'm going to make a very bold statement: *I believe it is impossible to consistently walk in obedience and holiness unless you have the fear of God in your heart.* If you don't have the fear of God, you will eventually believe that God is easy on sin. You'll think that you can sin all you want. You'll get on a merry-go-round of 'sin, confess, sin, confess'—and you'll say to yourself, 'I'll just run back to Jesus and make it right. He'll forgive me at any moment!'"[34]

How Do We Develop Fear of God?

Fear of God comes from knowledge of God. The greater our knowledge of God, the greater our fear of God. Proverbs 1:7 says, "The fear of the LORD is the beginning of knowledge." In Deuteronomy 17:18–20 God commanded kings:

Also it shall be, when he sits on the throne of his kingdom, that he shall write for himself a copy of this law in a book, from the one before the priests, the Levites. And it shall be with him, and he shall read it all the days of his life, *that he may learn to fear the LORD his God and be careful to observe all the words of this law and these statutes*, that his heart may not be lifted above his brethren, *that he may not turn aside*

from the commandment to the right hand or to the left, and
that he may prolong his days in his kingdom, he
and his children in the midst of Israel.

Kings had plenty of servants, but God commanded
them to write a copy of the law for themselves. They had
to keep it with them and read it throughout their lives. The
result? They would "learn to fear God," which came from
their knowledge of God. Then they would "observe all the
words of [the] law" and "not turn aside from [obeying]."

In Revelation 1:14–17, John received a vision of the
glorified Christ:

His head and hair were white like wool, as white as
snow, and His eyes like a flame of fire; His feet
were like fine brass, as if refined in a furnace, and
His voice as the sound of many waters; He had in
His right hand seven stars, out of His mouth went a
sharp two-edged sword, and His countenance was
like the sun shining in its strength. And *when I saw
Him, I fell at His feet as dead.* But He laid His right
hand on me, saying to me, "Do not be afraid; I am
the First and the Last."

Something similar took place with Peter, James, and
John at the Transfiguration.[35] Matthew 17:2, 5–7 records:

[Jesus] was transfigured before them. His face shone
like the sun, and His clothes became as white as the
light... A bright cloud overshadowed them; and

suddenly a voice came out of the cloud, saying, "This is My beloved Son, in whom I am well pleased. Hear Him!" And when the disciples heard it, *they fell on their faces and were greatly afraid.* But Jesus came and touched them and said, "Arise, and do not be afraid."

These visions provide an excellent knowledge of Jesus because they reveal His glory. Throughout Jesus' earthly life His glory was veiled, but the Transfiguration was the one instance He allowed it to shine forth. During the rest of His earthly life, He was physically the Son of Man, but at the Transfiguration, He revealed Himself as the Son of God. The knowledge of who Jesus is caused the witnesses to collapse in fear. So great was the fear created that in both accounts Jesus tenderly touched them and offered encouraging words.

If we saw the glorified Christ, the fear of Him would create greater obedience throughout the rest of our lives. When you know the God of the Bible—His "goodness and severity" (Romans 11:22)—how can you not be motivated to obey Him? Hebrews 12:28–29 says, "Serve God acceptably with reverence and godly fear. For our God is a consuming fire." The author of Hebrews motivated his readers to service and obedience with imagery that drives fear into all but the most foolish people.

Was Abraham Wise or Foolish?

If people knew what Abraham planned to do with Isaac, which words might they use to describe his actions? Foolish, irrational, and even evil, but Abraham's actions were wise. Regardless of how it looks to others, obedience always demonstrates wisdom. God said, "Observe [My commands and statutes] carefully, for *this will show your wisdom and understanding to the nations*, who will hear about all these decrees and say, 'Surely *this great nation is a wise and understanding people*'" (Deuteronomy 4:6 NIV). Israel's obedience to God even demonstrated their wisdom and understanding to the surrounding pagan nations.

Proverbs 9:10 says, "Fear of the LORD is the beginning of wisdom, and the knowledge of the Holy One is understanding." Psalm 111:10 says, "The fear of the LORD is the beginning of wisdom; a good understanding have all those who do His commandments." Fear of the Lord demonstrates wisdom and understanding because it reveals a heart that fears God. Disobedience shows foolishness because it uncovers a heart that does not fear God. Regardless of the education and degrees people have, if they do not fear God, they have no wisdom.

Questions

1. Do you feel motivated to obey God because of your love for Him, your fear of Him, or both? Explain your answer.

2. Provide two scriptural examples of people who exhibited fear of God through obedience.

3. Provide two examples from Scripture of people who showed a lack of fear of God through disobedience.

4. How does fear of God "[perfect] holiness" in us as described in 2 Corinthians 7:1?

5. Which verses or accounts in Scripture cause you to fear God?

6. How does obeying God demonstrate wisdom? How does disobeying Him demonstrate foolishness?

Chapter 9

God Prepares His People

After discussing Abraham's great faith and the wisdom he demonstrated through his obedience, we might feel discouraged because we are not more like him. But God prepared Abraham for the test in Genesis 22, and it should be an encouragement that He also prepares us for the trials and tests we face.

God Prepared Abraham through Their Relationship

By the time Genesis 22 takes place, Abraham had a deep history with God. Abraham had been through many experiences with God, and as a result, he knew Him. When Abraham interceded for Sodom, he talked God down from fifty righteous people to ten righteous people (Genesis

18:32). The exchange looked like a conversation between friends, which is fitting since three times in Scripture Abraham is called God's friend (2 Chronicles 20:7; Isaiah 41:8; James 2:23). At points, Abraham worried about pushing God too far, but the longer they talked, the more Abraham learned about God's patience and graciousness. Experiences in relationships can allow trust to build. Abraham had been through so much with God that he trusted Him, even when He asked him to sacrifice his son.

When Abraham first met God back in Genesis 12, could he have passed the same test he passed in Genesis 22? Did Abraham have the faith in Genesis 12 to do what he did in Genesis 22? I doubt it. God prepared Abraham for Genesis 22 in the previous ten chapters.

Abraham needed great faith to sacrifice Isaac, and God built that faith in Abraham through their relationship. For example, Abraham believed God would raise Isaac from the dead, and God convinced Abraham He could raise Isaac from the dead by bringing two other bodies back to life—his and Sarah's. Abraham knew he and Sarah could no longer have children. Their bodies were "dead," but Romans 4:19–21 says:

> And not being weak in faith, [Abraham] did not consider his own body, *already dead* (since he was about a hundred years old), and *the deadness* of Sarah's womb. He did not waver at the promise of God through unbelief, but was strengthened in faith, giving glory to God, and being fully

convinced that what He had promised He was also able to perform.

Abraham believed God could raise Isaac from the dead. Why? He experienced God supernaturally raise his and Sarah's "dead" bodies in their old age so they could have Isaac.

God Prepared Abraham through Previous Tests

God also prepared Abraham for the test of Genesis 22 through the tests He gave him in the previous chapters. Genesis 12:1 records:

> Now the LORD had said to Abram: "Get out of
> your country, from your family and from your
> father's house, to a land that I will show you."

This is the "Family Test" that involved leaving his relatives behind. Abraham failed by bringing his nephew, Lot. At the same time, Abraham faced the "Walk by Faith Test" since God told him to go to a land he had never seen. Abraham passed this test, and then he faced the "Famine Test." Genesis 12:10 says:

> Now there was a famine in the land, and Abram
> went down to Egypt to dwell there, for the famine
> was severe in the land.

Abraham failed this test when he left the land and went to Egypt. Then he also failed the "Fear of Man Test" when he told Sarah to say she was his sister to protect himself: "Please say you are my sister, that it may be well with me for your sake, and that I may live because of you" (Genesis 12:13).

In Genesis 13, Abraham passed the "Generosity Test." His herdsmen began fighting with Lot's herdsmen, and Abraham gave Lot the best choice of land for his animals. Genesis 13:8–9 records:

> So Abram said to Lot, "Please let there be no strife between you and me, and between my herdsmen and your herdsmen; for we are brethren. Is not the whole land before you? Please separate from me. If you take the left, then I will go to the right; or, if you go to the right, then I will go to the left."

In Genesis 14, Abraham passed the "Compassion Test" when he risked his life to rescue his nephew Lot from the five kings who captured him. Genesis 14:14 and 16 record:

> Now when Abram heard that [Lot] was taken captive, he armed his three hundred and eighteen trained servants who were born in his own house, and went in pursuit as far as Dan… So he brought back all the goods, and [Lot] and his goods.

Then Abraham passed the "Giving Test" when he would not keep the wealth he acquired from the battle against Sodom. Genesis 14:21–23 records:

> Now the king of Sodom said to Abram, "Give me the persons, and take the goods for yourself." But Abram said to the king of Sodom, "I have raised my hand to the LORD, God Most High, the Possessor of heaven and earth, that I will take nothing, from a thread to a sandal strap, and that I will not take anything that is yours, lest you should say, 'I have made Abram rich.'"

Abraham failed the "Spiritual Leader Test" when he submitted to Sarah and had a child with Hagar. Genesis 16:1–2 records:

> Now Sarai, Abram's wife, had borne him no children. And she had an Egyptian maidservant whose name was Hagar. So Sarai said to Abram, "See now, the LORD has restrained me from bearing children. Please, go in to my maid; perhaps I shall obtain children by her." And Abram heeded the voice of Sarai.

Abraham passed the "Circumcision Test" when God gave him the sign of the covenant, and he had the males with him obey. Genesis 17:23 says:

So Abraham took Ishmael his son, all who were born in his house and all who were bought with his money, every male among the men of Abraham's house, and circumcised the flesh of their foreskins that very same day, as God had said to him.

Abraham failed the "Integrity Test" when he lied about Sarah being his sister. Genesis 20:2 says, "Now Abraham said of Sarah his wife, 'She is my sister.' And Abimelech king of Gerar sent and took Sarah." He put his wife in danger, and she ended up in a pagan king's harem.

Finally, Abraham passed the "Ishmael Test" that most clearly prepared him for Genesis 22. God commanded him to give up a different son. This test is overshadowed by the account with Isaac, but it was still very difficult for Abraham. Genesis 21:9–14 records:

Sarah saw the son of Hagar the Egyptian, whom she had borne to Abraham, scoffing. Therefore she said to Abraham, "Cast out this bondwoman and her son; for the son of this bondwoman shall not be heir with my son, namely with Isaac." And *the matter was very displeasing in Abraham's sight* because of his son.
But God said to Abraham, "*Do not let it be displeasing in your sight* because of the lad or because of your bondwoman. Whatever Sarah has said to you, listen to her voice; for in Isaac your seed shall be called. Yet I will also make a nation of the son of the

bondwoman, because he is your seed."
So Abraham rose early in the morning, and took
bread and a skin of water; and putting it on her
shoulder, he gave it and the boy to Hagar, and sent
her away. Then she departed and wandered in the
Wilderness of Beersheba.

Twice Abraham's "displeasure" is mentioned, but he
still passed the test. Before God ever asked Abraham to
offer up Isaac, He first asked him to "offer up" Ishmael.
Did Abraham have any idea God would soon after say,
"Take now your son, your only son Isaac, whom you love,
and offer him as a burnt offering"? No, but God prepared
him for that difficult test through the previous tests.

God Prepared David through Previous Tests

Abraham was far from the only person in the Old
Testament God tested. David faced a great test when he
went before Goliath. Although it would be terrifying,
David did not seem the least bit afraid. First Samuel 17:45–
47 records:

Then David said to the Philistine, "You come to
me with a sword, with a spear, and with a javelin.
But I come to you in the name of the LORD of
hosts, the God of the armies of Israel, whom you
have defied. This day the LORD will deliver you into
my hand, and I will strike you and take your head

from you. And this day I will give the carcasses of
the camp of the Philistines to the birds of the air
and the wild beasts of the earth, that all the earth
may know that there is a God in Israel. Then all
this assembly shall know that the LORD does not
save with sword and spear; for the battle is the
LORD's, and He will give you into our hands."

Why was David so confident he could defeat Goliath?
He provided the answer before he stepped on the
battlefield. When Saul discouraged David from fighting
Goliath, David responded with such a convincing
argument that Saul permitted him. First Samuel 17:34–37
records:

David said to Saul, "Your servant used to keep his
father's sheep, and when a lion or a bear came and
took a lamb out of the flock, I went out after it and
struck it, and delivered the lamb from its mouth;
and when it arose against me, I caught it by its
beard, and struck and killed it. Your servant has
killed both lion and bear; and this uncircumcised
Philistine will be like one of them, seeing he has
defied the armies of the living God. The LORD,
Who delivered me from the paw of the lion and
from the paw of the bear, He will deliver me from
the hand of this Philistine."

David experienced earlier tests with lions and bears that
prepared him for the test with Goliath. David was

confident God would deliver him from Goliath because of God's previous deliverances. God spent years delivering David, and that convinced him He would similarly deliver him from Goliath. God's past faithfulness gave David confidence in God's future faithfulness.

God Prepares Us through Previous Tests

Sometimes people read the Old Testament and think, "What does this have to do with me? How can I learn from people whose lives are so different from mine?" These are unfortunate questions because the New Testament states the Old Testament provides us with examples:

- Romans 15:4—"For whatever things were written [in the Old Testament] were written *for our learning.*"
- 1 Corinthians 10:11—"Now all these things happened to [the Israelites] *as examples*, and they were written *for our admonition.*"

Church age believers can learn from Old Testament accounts which often provide a backdrop for New Testament instruction. Abraham and David's lives are instructive because God tests us like He tested them. When Abraham and David passed the tests they faced, it proved the genuineness of their faith. First Peter 1:7 says "the genuineness of [our] faith [is shown when] it is tested."

Also, just as God did with Abraham and David, He uses the previous chapters of our lives to write our future chapters. The previous tests prepare us for future tests. As Abraham and David looked to God's past faithfulness to be confident in His future faithfulness, we must look to God's past faithfulness to be confident in His continued faithfulness to us.

The Danger of Forgetting God's Past Faithfulness

Israel faced a difficult test when entering the Promised Land. They had many enemies to defeat, and God prepared them by dramatically defeating their previous enemy— Egypt. Israel focused on God's victory over Egypt, and so—with only a few exceptions—the Book of Joshua is a record of their victories over the Canaanites. Surprisingly though, Israel then moved to a record of failures in the book of Judges. Why the dramatic change? They forgot God's past faithfulness, and failed terribly as a result. Judges 2:7, 10–12 records:

> So the people served the LORD all the days of Joshua, and all the days of the elders who outlived Joshua, who had seen all the great works of the LORD which He had done for Israel… When all that generation had been gathered to their fathers, another generation arose after them *who did not know the LORD nor the work which He had done for Israel.* Then the children of Israel did evil in the sight of the LORD, and served the Baals; and they forsook

the LORD God of their fathers, Who had brought them out of the land of Egypt; and they followed other gods from among the gods of the people who were all around them, and they bowed down to them; and they provoked the LORD to anger.

The Israelites in Judges failed because they "did not know the LORD nor the work which He had done." The old generation from Joshua's day knew God and what He had done, but the new generation did not know God any better than they knew the gods of the Canaanites. Thus, it was easy for them to "[serve] the Baals [and forsake] the LORD God of their fathers...and follow other gods from among the [Canaanites]." We must do two things to avoid the same failure in our lives!

First, we know God through the Bible. It is His record of Himself. People who do not know the God of the Bible will be about as successful against the tests they face as the Israelites were in Judges. To have confidence in God's past faithfulness, we must know His past faithfulness, and it is recorded for us in Scripture. God wants us to know Him so we can trust Him, but people who do not know God cannot trust Him. If you want to be able to trust God when tested, then learn from the Word that He is a God Who can be trusted.

Second, Abraham and David passed tests they faced, because of their relationships with God. But the Israelites in Judges had no relationships with God. We must seek the Lord when we face tests, so we can build relationships with

Him. Some people do not expect God to deliver in the future because they never sought His deliverance in the past. People can only trust God's future faithfulness if they know His past faithfulness, and people can only know God's past faithfulness if He has been part of their pasts. If we expect to be able to trust God in the future, we must seek Him in the present to build a history with Him.

Questions

1. Why was Abraham able to obey God despite the great difficulty involved?

2. What steps can you take to strengthen your relationship with God?

3. In what ways did God prepare Abraham for the test in Genesis 22?

4. Provide three other scriptural examples of God preparing people for tests.

5. In what ways has God prepared you for tests in your life?

6. What are three common reasons in Scripture that people disobey God?

7. What are three common reasons in your life that you disobey God?

8. Why is it important to remember God's past faithfulness?

9. Why is it important to pass on the knowledge of God to the next generation? Aside from the Book of Judges, can you think of two examples of that happening?

Chapter 10

The Lamb That Makes
Christianity the Opposite

Genesis 22:8—And Abraham said, "My son, *God will provide for Himself the lamb* for a burnt offering." So the two of them went together.

braham's words seem absurd. God would provide a lamb for the sacrifice to Him? Religion is about what man does. That is what makes it worship—man brings something that will please; man offers something to appease. At the heart of other religions are individuals bringing sacrifices to the false gods they worship, but at the heart of Christianity is a God Who provides the sacrifice Himself. This does not just make Christianity different than other religions; it makes Christianity the *opposite* of other religions.

Propitiation is a wonderful word, but it lacks use in the English language and, unfortunately, is even removed from some Bible versions. Propitiation is a two-part act that involves 1. turning away the wrath of an offended individual and 2. being reconciled to the person as a result. Close synonyms are appeasing, expiating, placating, and satisfying.

In other religions, man accomplishes the propitiation through the sacrifice he provides, but in Christianity, God accomplished the propitiation through the Sacrifice He provided. His wrath was turned away from believers because it was poured out on His Son. We are reconciled to God because of what He did for us: "When we were enemies we were reconciled to God through the death of His Son" (Romans 5:10a). Thus, the four times the New Testament uses the word propitiation it refers to what God did for man, and not what man does for God:

- Romans 3:25— "[Jesus] Whom *God set forth as a propitiation* by His blood."
- Hebrews 2:17—"In all things He had to be made like His brethren, that He might be a merciful and faithful High Priest in things pertaining to God, to *make propitiation for the sins of the people.*"
- 1 John 2:2—"*He Himself is the propitiation for our sins*, and not for ours only but also for the whole world."
- 1 John 4:10—"In this is love, not that we loved God, but that He loved us and *sent His Son to be the propitiation for our sins.*"

Only God could provide a perfect sacrifice that would appease Him. Isaiah 53:11 says, "He shall see the labor of His soul, and *be satisfied.*" The "labor" refers to Jesus' suffering on the cross, and it "satisfied" God.

In Hebrews 10:5, Jesus said, "Sacrifice and offering You did not desire, but a body You have prepared for Me." God did not desire the sacrifices and offerings in the Old Testament, but Jesus' perfect, sinless "body" could appease Him. As the lyrics of "In Christ Alone" state, "'Til on that cross as Jesus died, the wrath of God was satisfied."[36]

To go a step further, not only did God provide the Sacrifice, He *became* the Sacrifice. If we made propitiation for our sins, it would be about us and what we did for God. We could proudly take credit for our salvation. With God accomplishing the propitiation from beginning to end— providing and becoming the sacrifice—it is about Him and what He has done for us. He receives the praise and honor.

The Tower of Babel—A Picture of False, Works-Based Religions

The Tower of Babel was the first organized rebellion against God. Genesis 11:3–4 records:

> Then they said to one another, "Come, *let us* make bricks and bake them thoroughly... Come, *let us* build ourselves a city, and a tower whose top is in

the heavens; *let us make a name for ourselves*, lest we be scattered abroad over the face of the whole earth."

In false religions, people reach up to God offering sacrifices that amount to nothing. They spend their lives piling one brick on top of another, but they do not get any closer to heaven than the people who constructed the Tower of Babel. Three times they said, "Let us," and their pride and self-focus is revealed through their desire to "make a name for [themselves]" versus God. Genesis 11:5–7 records:

> But *the* LORD *came down* to see the city and the tower
> which the sons of men had built. And the LORD
> said, "Indeed the people are one and they all have
> one language, and this is what they begin to do;
> now nothing that they propose to do will be
> withheld from them. Come, *let Us go down* and there
> confuse their language, that they may not
> understand one another's speech."

This is a dramatic reversal! Man said, "Let us build [to] the heavens…" but then God said, "Let Us go down…" referring to all three Persons: God the Father, God the Son, and God the Holy Spirit. The language of God "coming down" is a theme throughout the Old Testament:

- God saw the wickedness of Sodom and Gomorrah and said, "*I will go down* now and see whether they have done altogether according to the outcry against it that has come to Me; and if not, I will know" (Genesis 18:21).

- When Israel was in slavery in Egypt God said, "So *I have come down* to deliver them out of the hand of the Egyptians, and to bring them up from that land to a good and large land, to a land flowing with milk and honey" (Exodus 3:8).
- The psalmist said, "He bowed the heavens also, and *came down* with darkness under His feet" (Psalm 18:9; see also Psalm 144:5).

The description of God coming down is not as literal as it sounds. God did not leave heaven to see what was happening at the Tower of Babel, Sodom and Gomorrah, or when Israel was in Egypt as though He did not know. This language shows God's interest and intervention in man's affairs. This is another difference between Christianity and other religions. False gods are often aloof, stoic, and uninterested in man's affairs. The God of the Bible is deeply concerned and involved.

Examples of God "coming down" take place soon after Israel was delivered from Egypt. He came down to Sinai:

- Exodus 19:11—"And let them be ready for the third day. For on the third day *the LORD will come down* upon Mount Sinai in the sight of all the people."
- Exodus 19:18–20—"Now Mount Sinai was completely in smoke, because *the LORD descended* upon it in fire. Its smoke ascended like the smoke of

a furnace, and the whole mountain quaked greatly. And when the blast of the trumpet sounded long and became louder and louder, Moses spoke, and God answered him by voice. Then *the LORD came down* upon Mount Sinai, on the top of the mountain."

Then God came down to the Tent of Meeting, followed by the tabernacle (Exodus 40:34), and finally the temple (1 Kings 8:10). Exodus 33:9–11 records:

And it came to pass, when Moses entered the tabernacle, that *the pillar of cloud descended and stood at the door of the tabernacle, and the LORD talked with Moses.* All the people saw the pillar of cloud *standing at the tabernacle door*, and all the people rose and worshiped, each man in his tent door. So *the LORD spoke to Moses face to face, as a man speaks to his friend.*

Much of the language describes God as a man: "stood/standing at the door… talked with Moses." We are even told God spoke to Moses "as a man." This is *anthropomorphism* or ascribing human attributes to God. Other examples include God remembering (Genesis 8:1), smelling (Numbers 15:3), stretching out His hand (Psalm 136:12), making His face shine on us (Numbers 6:25), and opening His ears to our cries (Psalm 34:15). God does not literally forget and then need to remember, hold people's hand, or open His ears (as though there are other times He does not hear us). Instead, this language is used to help us relate to God and understand Him better.

This prefigured the incarnation. Jesus not only fulfilled the prophecies of His coming; He also fulfilled the Old Testament anthropomorphic imagery of God being a man and coming down from heaven to earth. The apostle Paul explained it this way in Philippians 2:6–8 (ESV):

> Though [Jesus] was in the form of God, He did not count equality with God a thing to be grasped, but emptied Himself, by taking the form of a servant, being born in the likeness of men. And *being found in human form*, he humbled himself by becoming obedient to the point of death, even death on a cross.

It is not just that Jesus came from heaven to earth; it is *how* He came. The Greek word for "emptied Himself" is *kenoō*, which is where we get the theological term, *kenosis*.[37] When God became a Man in the Person of Jesus Christ, He emptied Himself of certain rights and privileges:

- Omniscience—Jesus limited Himself to knowing only what the Father wanted Him to know. For example, the "day and hour" of His return was not something for Him to know during His earthly ministry (Mark 13:32).
- Eternal riches—Jesus' life on earth did not have the glory or majesty He knew in heaven. On earth He owned very little: "Though He was rich, yet for your sakes He became poor, that you through His poverty might become rich" (2 Corinthians 8:9).

- Honor—In heaven, He was loved and worshipped, but on earth, He was, "a reproach of men, and despised by the people" (Psalm 22:6; see also Isaiah 53:3). When "He came to His own... His own did not receive Him" (John 1:11).
- Glory—He did not look on earth as He looked in heaven: "Father, glorify Me together with Yourself, with the glory which I had with You before the world was" (John 17:5).

When discussing the kenosis, it is also important to understand what Jesus did not empty Himself of—deity. He did not stop being God. The words "taking the form" reveal an addition, not a subtraction. Jesus did not exchange deity for humanity. He added humanity to deity. He had two natures, human and divine, which are inseparable. He will forever be the God-Man. Not fifty-fifty, but 100 percent God and 100 percent man.

Jesus' entrance into the world gives credibility to Christianity because this is not the story man would write. This reveals another difference between Christianity and other religions. Would false gods be born in Bethlehem in a manger to a poor family with no-name parents? Is this how they would make their entrance into the world? Jesus "took the form of a servant." Would false gods of other religions come and serve? They would be served. Would they stoop down and wash people's feet? They would have people wash their feet. The Jews, who spent centuries looking forward to their Messiah, struggled with Jesus being the Christ because of His humility.

Paul used ever-increasing terms to describe Jesus as the Lamb that God would "provide for Himself"—Jesus "did not cling to equality with God... He emptied Himself... He became a Man... He was a Servant... He was obedient... even to death" (Philippians 2:6–8). But Paul did not stop at stating Jesus' death because it is not just that He died. It is *how* He died—the most shameful, agonizing death imaginable—"even death on a cross."

This is the bottom rung that God the Father needed His Son to reach for man to be saved; therefore, even at Jesus' birth, the focus is on His death. Matthew and Luke provide the records, and they do not focus on the world receiving a great teacher, miracle worker, prophet, or even king. Jesus was all these, but the focus is on the world receiving a Savior:

- Matthew 1:21—"And she will bring forth a Son, and you shall call His name Jesus, for *He will save His people from their sins.*"
- Luke 2:11—"For there is born to you this day in the city of David *a Savior*, Who is Christ the Lord."

When people think of Jesus, if they fail to see Him as the fulfillment of Abraham's words—the Lamb "God [provided] for Himself"—they fail to recognize why He came. They fail to see why Christianity is the opposite of other religions.

The Only Son God Recognizes

Three times (Genesis 22:2, 12, and 16), God said Isaac was Abraham's "only son." God wants to make sure we do not miss that Isaac was Abraham's "only son," but Abraham had another son—Ishmael. Why did God not acknowledge him? He was produced from unbelief instead of faith, and "whatever is not from faith is sin" (Romans 14:23). Ishmael was the result of Abraham and Sarah's works to fulfill God's promise, which God would not recognize. Ishmael is a picture of salvation by works—seeking to fulfill God's promise through human effort. The spiritual application is that as Abraham could not work to receive God's promised son, we cannot work to receive God's promised salvation:

- Romans 3:28 (ESV)—"A man is justified by faith *apart from works of the law.*"
- Ephesians 2:8–9—"For by grace you have been saved through faith, and that *not of yourselves*; it is the gift of God, *not of works*, lest anyone should boast."
- 2 Timothy 1:9—"[God] saved us… *not according to our works*, but according to His own purpose and grace which was given to us in Christ Jesus before time began"
- Titus 3:5—"*Not by works of righteousness which we have done*, but according to His mercy He saved us…"

God does not recognize our works for salvation any more than He recognized Ishmael. Aside from being ineffective, attempting to be saved by works also, produces one of two equally terrible outcomes. People say, "I can never be good enough," which produces despair, or "I have been good enough," which produces pride.

Ishmael illustrates working for salvation, and Galatians 4:30 quotes Genesis 21:10 to show he must be removed:

> Nevertheless what does the Scripture say? "Cast out the bondwoman (Hagar) and her son (Ishmael), for the son of the bondwoman *shall not be heir* with the son (Isaac) of the freewoman (Sarah)."

Since Ishmael was not a legitimate son, he could not receive the inheritance. Only Isaac could:

- Genesis 15:4—"The Lord [said to Abraham], 'This one (Ishmael) shall not be your heir, but one who will come from your own body (Isaac) shall be your heir.'"
- Genesis 21:10—"[Sarah] said to Abraham, 'Cast out this bondwoman and her son; for the son of this bondwoman shall not be heir with my son, namely with Isaac.'"

God recognized Isaac because he was the son of faith, and God recognizes us if we are sons of faith: "Therefore know that only those who are of faith are sons of

Abraham... For you are all sons of God through faith in Christ Jesus" (Galatians 3:7, 26).

In Genesis 26:3, God told Isaac, "Dwell in this land, and I will be with you and bless you; for *to you and your descendants I give all these lands*, and I will perform the oath which I swore to Abraham your father." Isaac was the heir, so he received the inheritance. We are heirs with Christ, so we share in the inheritance:

- Romans 8:17—"If children, then heirs—heirs of God and joint heirs with Christ."
- Galatians 3:29—"If you are Christ's, then you are Abraham's seed, and heirs according to the promise."

A Father offered His Son so people can become His sons and daughters. The work has been done. On the cross, Jesus said, "It is finished" (John 19:30). Have you recognized you are a sinner who cannot save himself/herself, and your works are building the Tower of Babel? Please do not finish this book without repenting of your sins and putting your faith in the Lamb God provided. He was willing to receive the punishment your sins deserve, so you would not have to experience that punishment—eternity in hell—yourself.

> 1 Timothy 1:15—"This is a faithful saying and worthy of all acceptance, **that Christ Jesus came into the world to save sinners**, of whom I am chief."

Questions

1. Although there are many differences between Christianity and other religions, explain the most important one.

2. Aside from the Tower of Babel, what other examples of false religion do you see in Scripture?

3. Why is it important that God, versus man, provided the sacrifice for mankind's salvation?

4. What is the motivating factor behind false religions?

5. How are false gods different than the God of the Bible?

6. What did Jesus "empty Himself" of at the incarnation?

7. What did Jesus not "empty Himself" of at the incarnation, and provide three verses to support your answer.

8. How does the contrasting account with Ishmael help us better understand God's plan of redemption?

9. In what way(s) are you working for salvation—trying to earn God's favor?

10. In what way(s) are you trusting God and walking by faith?

11. If you have repented and put your faith in Christ, provide three verses that give you confidence in your salvation.

12. If you have not repented and put your faith in Christ, what is hindering you? Are you confused or afraid? Do you have questions? If I can help you, please reach out to me personally at scott@scottlapierre.org.

About the Author

Scott is the senior pastor of Woodland Christian Church in Woodland, Washington and a conference speaker. He and his wife, Katie, grew up together in northern California, and God has blessed them with seven children.

You can contact Pastor Scott or learn more about him at the following:

- Email: scott@scottlapierre.org
- Website: www.scottlapierre.org
- Facebook: @ScottLaPierreAuthor
- YouTube: @ScottLaPierre
- Twitter: @PastorWCC
- Instagram: @PastorWCC

Receive FREE chapters of Pastor Scott's books and videos of his conference messages by subscribing to his newsletter:

https://www.scottlapierre.org/subscribe/

Would You Like to Invite Pastor Scott to Speak at Your Event?

You can expect:

- Professionally prepared and delivered messages
- Handouts with lessons and discussion questions
- Copies of Pastor Scott's books to offer as gifts to increase registrations (if you desire)
- Prompt replies to communication
- Advertising of your event on Pastor Scott's social media

Schedule for Conferences—typically there are one or two sessions on Friday evening and three or four sessions on Saturday, but there is flexibility. Conferences can be spread over three days or kept to one day, and Q&A sessions can be added.

Outreach—consider viewing the conference as an outreach to share Christ with your community. Pastor Scott can run a Facebook ad, and/or set up a Facebook event page for those in the church to share with others.

For more information, including sample messages and endorsements, please visit:

www.scottlapierre.org/conferences-and-speaking.

Marriage God's Way:
A Biblical Recipe for Healthy,
Joyful, Christ-Centered Relationships

Nearly everything in life comes with instructions, from the cell phones we use to the automobiles we drive. Yet when it comes to marriage, many  people struggle without proper guidance. Couples experience pain and conflict when love and joy should flourish. The good news is there are instructions for marriage too, written by the One who created marriage. In *Marriage God's Way,* whether you are preparing for your wedding, newlyweds, or marriage veterans, you will learn these biblical instructions.

Marriage God's Way has been endorsed by well-known ministry leaders:

- **Tedd Tripp**: "The reader will be richly rewarded."
  —Best-selling author of *Shepherding a Child's Heart*
- **Scott Brown**: "This is what every marriage needs!"
  —President of The National Center for Family-Integrated Churches and author of *A Theology of the Family*

Enduring Trials God's Way:
A Biblical Recipe for Finding Joy in Suffering

Trials are part of life on this side of
heaven, and God wants to use them
for your good! Learn scriptural
principles that give you the
encouragement you need when
suffering. Every chapter concludes
with questions that help you apply what you are reading.

- Develop the spiritual perspective to embrace trials
- Appreciate the maturity trials produce
- Understand the rewards for enduring trials
- Recognize God is still compassionate and gracious
  during trials

Enduring Trials God's Way has been endorsed by well-
known ministry leaders:

- **Douglas Bond:** "Richly biblical and encouraging,
  Scott LaPierre's latest book reveals a gracious
  pastor's heart, compassionately equipping people
  for trials. Every believer needs this book!"
  —Speaker, tour leader, and author
- **Dr. Carlton McLeod:** "One of the best biblical
  treatments of suffering I have seen. You want this
  book in your library!"
  —Speaker, author, and senior pastor

Notes

[1] "353 Prophecies Fulfilled in Jesus Christ." http://www.accordingtothescriptures.org/prophecy/353 prophecies.html

[2] "G3847 - parabasis – Strong's Greek Lexicon (KJV)." Blue Letter Bible. Accessed 6 Jul, 2018. https://www.blueletterbible.org//lang/Lexicon/Lexicon. cfm?Strongs=G3847&t=KJV

[3] "H7535 - raq – Strong's Hebrew Lexicon (NKJV)." Blue Letter Bible. Accessed 11 Jul, 2018. https://www.blueletterbible.org//lang/lexicon/lexicon.c fm?Strongs=H7535&t=NKJV

[4] "H389 – 'ak – Strong's Hebrew Lexicon (NKJV)." Blue Letter Bible. Accessed 11 Jul, 2018. https://www.blueletterbible.org//lang/lexicon/lexicon.c fm?Strongs=H389&t=NKJV

[5] "H3173 - yachiyd – Strong's Hebrew Lexicon (KJV)." Blue Letter Bible. Accessed 6 Jul, 2018. https://www.blueletterbible.org//lang/Lexicon/Lexicon. cfm?Strongs=H3173&t=KJV

[6] *The Theological Wordbook of the Old Testament* (TWoT) R. Laird Harris, editor, Gleason L. Archer, Jr., associate editor, Bruce K. Waltke, associate editor. Chicago: Moody

Press, 1980. Deals with Hebrew/Aramaic words in the Old Testament that have a theological significance.

[7] Along with the Apostles' Creed, the Nicene Creed is the most universally accepted statement of the Christian Faith. The Roman Emperor Constantine convened the Council of Nicea to try to unify the Christian church with one doctrine, especially regarding the Trinity and deity of Jesus. The Nicene Creed was adopted at the council in A.D. 325. For further information, visit: https://www.gotquestions.org/Nicene-creed.html

[8] "G3439 - monogenēs – Strong's Greek Lexicon (KJV)." Blue Letter Bible. Accessed 6 Jul, 2018. https://www.blueletterbible.org//lang/lexicon/lexicon.cfm?Strongs=g3439&t=kjv

[9] "What Is the Law of First Mention?" Got Questions. https://www.gotquestions.org/law-of-first-mention.html. Accessed 20 Aug, 2018.

[10] "H5927 - `alah – Strong's Hebrew Lexicon (NKJV)." Blue Letter Bible. Accessed 11 Jul, 2018. https://www.blueletterbible.org//lang/lexicon/lexicon.cfm?Strongs=H5927&t=NKJV

[11] The parallel account in Chronicles says "Ornan," which is a variant of "Araunah."

[12] "H4179 - Mowriyah – Strong's Hebrew Lexicon (KJV)." Blue Letter Bible. Accessed 6 Jul, 2018. https://www.blueletterbible.org//lang/Lexicon/Lexicon.cfm?Strongs=H4179&t=KJV

[13] Barker, Kenneth L. and John R. Kohlenberger III. *Expositor's Bible Commentary – Abridged Edition Old Testament.* Zondervan, 2017.

[14] Earle, Ralph. Adam Clarke's Commentary on the Bible – Abridged. Word Publishing 1997. p. 712.

[15] "G3850 - parabolē – Strong's Greek Lexicon (NKJV)." Blue Letter Bible. Accessed 14 Jul, 2018. https://www.blueletterbible.org//lang/lexicon/lexicon.cfm?Strongs=G3850&t=NKJV

[16] *The Moody Bible Commentary: A One-Volume Commentary on the Whole* Bible by the Faculty of Moody Bible Institute. Moody Publishers, 2014. p. 81.

[17] "H5288 – na'ar – Strong's Hebrew Lexicon (NKJV)." Blue Letter Bible. Accessed 17 Jul, 2018. https://www.blueletterbible.org//lang/lexicon/lexicon.cfm?Strongs=H5288&t=NKJV

[18] Zuck, Roy B. *Basic Bible Interpretation.* David C Cook. (April 1, 2002) p. 117.

[19] "G2316 - theos – Strong's Greek Lexicon (KJV)." Blue Letter Bible. Accessed 6 Jul, 2018. https://www.blueletterbible.org//lang/lexicon/lexicon.cfm?Strongs=g2316&t=kjv

[20] "G5316 - phainō – Strong's Greek Lexicon (KJV)." Blue Letter Bible. Accessed 6 Jul, 2018. https://www.blueletterbible.org//lang/lexicon/lexicon.cfm?Strongs=g5316&t=kjv

[21] Borland, James A. *Christ in the Old Testament: Old Testament Appearances of Christ in Human Form,* Chicago: Moody, 1978.

[22] See Genesis 16:7–23, 21:17–18, 22:11–18; Judges 2:1–4, 5:23, 6:11–14; 2 Samuel 24:16; Zechariah 1:12, 3:1, 12:8

[23] "H7716 - seh – Strong's Hebrew Lexicon (NKJV)." Blue Letter Bible. Accessed 23 Jul, 2018. https://www.blueletterbible.org//lang/lexicon/lexicon.cfm?Strongs=H7716&t=NKJV

[24] "H352 – 'ayil – Strong's Hebrew Lexicon (NKJV)." Blue Letter Bible. Accessed 23 Jul, 2018. https://www.blueletterbible.org//lang/lexicon/lexicon.cfm?Strongs=H352&t=NKJV

[25] Burnt offerings were discussed in Chapter Two.

[26] Matthew Henry, "Commentary on Genesis 22:11–14." Christian Classics Ethereal Library. http://www.ccel.org/ccel/henry/mhc1.Gen.xxiii.html. Accessed 20 Aug, 2018.

[27] Wiersbe, Warren. *The Bible Exposition Commentary, Volume I: Matthew–Galatians.* Chariot Victor Publishing, 2003, p. 323.

[28] Pink, A.W. Commentary on John 8:4. "A.W. Pink's Commentary on John and Hebrews." https://www.studylight.org/commentaries/awp/john-8.html.

[29] *The Moody Bible Commentary: A One-Volume Commentary on the Whole Bible* by the Faculty of Moody Bible Institute. Moody Publishers, 2014, p. 1634.

[30] Barnes, Albert, *Notes on the Bible*, by Albert Barnes, [1834], at sacred-texts.com http://www.sacred-texts.com/bib/cmt/barnes/joh008.htm

[31] Matthew Poole, Annotations Upon The Holy Bible: Wherein The Sacred Text Is Inserted, And Various Readings Annexed, Together With The Parallel Scriptures. Nabu Press, 2011, p. 105.

[32] Gill, John. *Exposition of the Old and New Testament*, by John Gill, [1746–63], at sacred-texts.com http://www.sacred-texts.com/bib/cmt/gill/joh008.htm

[33] "H461 – 'Eliy`ezer – Strong's Hebrew Lexicon (KJV)." Blue Letter Bible. Accessed 20 Aug, 2018. https://www.blueletterbible.org//lang/Lexicon/Lexicon.cfm?Strongs=H461&t=KJV

[34] Wilkerson, David. "Love, Fear, and Obedience." World Challenge. August 17, 1992. https://worldchallenge.org/newsletter/1992/love-fear-and-obedience

[35] For similar responses, see also Genesis 17:3, Numbers 16:22, Ezekiel 1:28, and Acts 9:4.

[36] "In Christ Alone." https://www.lyrics.com/lyric/9783521/Avalon/In+Christ+Alone

[37] "G2758 - kenoō – Strong's Greek Lexicon (ESV)." Blue Letter Bible. Accessed 28 Jul, 2018. https://www.blueletterbible.org//lang/lexicon/lexicon.cfm?Strongs=G2758&t=ESV

Made in United States
Troutdale, OR
01/10/2025

27823885R00105